VEGETABLES AND HERBS
FOR THE GREENHOUSE
AND POLYTUNNEL

Also in Right Way

Vegetable Growing Month by Month
The Essential Allotment Guide
Vegetable, Fruit and Herb Growing in Small Spaces
How to Store Your Home Grown Produce
Backgarden Chickens and Other Poultry
The Right Way to Keep Chickens

VEGETABLES AND HERBS FOR THE GREENHOUSE AND POLYTUNNEL

Klaus Laitenberger

RIGHT WAY

Constable & Robinson Ltd
55–56 Russell Square
London
WC1B 4HP
www.constablerobinson.com

Originally published as *Vegetables for the Polytunnel and Greenhouse*
by Milkwood Farm Publishing 2012
First published by Right Way, an imprint of Constable & Robinson, 2013

Illustrations by Dympna Driscoll
Victorian Images Courtesy of Thomas Etty Seeds Esq.

A copy of the British Library Cataloguing in Publication Data
is available from the British Library

ISBN: 978-0-7160-2342-5

Printed and bound in the EU

1 3 5 7 9 10 8 6 4 2

To forget how to dig the earth
and to tend the soil
is to forget ourselves

Mahatma Gandi

For Iris

CONTENTS

INTRODUCTION

I have always been passionate about growing food – all kinds of it – and I have never liked buying food that could be grown in my own garden. Unfortunately in our climate in western Europe there is a whole range of common vegetables that will do poorly outdoors and we need the extra heat and shelter of a greenhouse or polytunnel to get a good crop. Our growing season is very short but with the help of an indoor space we can prolong the production period for all vegetables. We can get an 'extra early' as well as an 'extra late' crop of most vegetables.

I promise you that getting a tunnel or a greenhouse will revolutionize your gardening life. It will open up new avenues, you'll experiment with new vegetables and you'll be guaranteed a food supply throughout the year. A friend of mine has even an armchair and a radio in his little greenhouse and uses it as his escape. Even if we get a poor summer you can get the illusion that you are in a different country and enjoy the warmth at home.

This book is aimed at anybody who has the wish to grow their own food and I'm hoping to encourage readers to experiment. Try out new vegetables, new varieties, new plants that you've never heard of or plants that we commonly use (soya beans, peanuts, ginger) but have never seen growing. This is the fun and excitement of gardening.

I made a conscious decision not to include the technical aspects of erecting a greenhouse or tunnel because there are plenty of excellent instructive manuals available. I'm a gardener who loves to grow food and I want to show you how simple it is to become more or less self-sufficient in fresh food. Growing your own food will also give you a sense of purpose and a sense of pride.

For each vegetable you'll find very detailed growing instructions. I'm an organic gardener and these have worked for me for many years but should not be viewed as a general rule. We all know that each gardener has different growing techniques and you'll find out your own best way.

Some people have reservations about polytunnels – the aesthetics as well as the use of plastic. Obviously most greenhouses are visually more pleasant than polytunnels but unfortunately more expensive unless you can build your own. Even with plastic for the tunnel covering I think it's a lot more environmentally friendly to grow your own fresh organic vegetables in a tunnel rather than importing them from all over the world, for example garlic from China and peas from Peru. In fact, over 80 per cent of all fresh organic vegetables are imported and most of them could be grown here.

Be warned though, once you have tasted your first home-grown tomato there is no way of going back to the factory farmed, sterile Dutch supermarket tomatoes that will never rot, bruise or crack and never taste of anything more than water.

Throughout the book I recommend varieties that I have found the very best in terms of flavour and natural healthy growth. I'm an experimenter by nature, but throughout the years of trials I have limited the range of varieties to just a few but this should not stop you from trying out new things. One year I grew 100 varieties of tomatoes in a large polytunnel and all the visitors had to do a taste test. The variety that came out on top was 'Sungold F1'. There is really no better tomato than 'Sungold F1'. You haven't fully lived until you've actually eaten one. Unfortunately it will hardly ever find its way into shops or supermarkets because it cracks and bruises easily. It needs to be eaten fresh from the plant.

I hope that this book will be useful for beginners and experienced gardeners alike and that you will soon discover with the help of a tunnel or greenhouse how easy it is to produce good, healthy food for your table. What greater satisfaction can there be?

It is quite amazing how many people are taking up vegetable growing again. In Ireland, where I live, I'm a patron of GIY (Grow it Yourself), an excellent non-profit organisation, which promotes growing your own food and showing people how to do it (www.giyireland.com).

AUBERGINE

Latin name: *Solanum melongena*
Family: *Solanaceae*

Aubergines have been cultivated in Asia since the fifth century BC. They were introduced to Spain by Arab conquerors in the fourth century AD. By the sixth century they were grown throughout Europe but mainly as an ornamental plant.

Aubergines are known as eggplants in America because the fruits of some varieties resemble eggs. Aubergines come in a wide range of colours, ranging from white, pink, red, purple to black. The shape of the fruit is also variable. It may be egg shaped, elongated or even finger like.

Unfortunately aubergines are a far less reliable crop compared to tomatoes and cucumbers. There is, however, always a space for one or two plants and the flavour of the fruit makes it all worthwhile. The secret of growing good aubergines is to start the seeds off early in the year and to choose a good variety.

SOIL AND SITE

Aubergines benefit from good ventilation so you may plant them close to the entrance. They require a fertile soil so plenty of mature compost or well rotted manure should be incorporated.

SOWING

Aubergines should be started off very early in the year as they require a long growing season. The best time to sow the seeds is from mid February until mid March at the latest. I usually sow the seeds in a small standard seed tray or pot and space the seeds about 2cm apart from each other. The tray should be placed into a warm propagator or on a warm windowsill. The temperature should be around 18–21°C. The seedlings start to appear within 7–10 days. About a week after they have germinated they should be pricked out into 7cm pots using potting compost. About 3–4 weeks later they can be potted on into a 10cm pot.

PLANTING

Aubergines are very sensitive to cold temperatures so they can only be planted into the greenhouse or tunnel in early May in mild areas or mid to late May in cooler districts.

SPACING

- Between plants: 45cm.
- Between rows: 45cm.

PLANT CARE

Apart from regular watering there is little else you need to do. If the plants grow too upright you can pinch out the growing shoot at about 50cm height. This encourages the plants to become more bushy. The plants usually require a single stake for support and heavy individual branches may be propped up with y-shaped sticks or tree branches.

Fig. 1. Aubergine branch propped up with a y-stick.

HARVESTING

Harvest the fruits when they are of the required size. The fruits should be shiny. If they turn pale it means that they are over mature and will taste tough. You can expect to get between 5 and 12 fruits per plant. The modern hybrid varieties will yield twice as many as some of the older types.

POTENTIAL PROBLEMS

Unfortunately aubergines are very prone to aphid attacks especially from the greenhouse whitefly and greenfly. The red spider mite may also present problems. Blossom end rot may be caused by irregular watering. As a prevention you can use a garlic or seaweed spray on a regular basis (every 10 days) throughout the whole growing season. This will prevent aphid attacks and will also strengthen your plants. Grey mould (botrytis) may also affect the plants. Use a milk/water mix (1:5) to cure the problem.

HOW MUCH TO GROW?

I never plant more than 3 plants, enough for an occasional treat.

VARIETIES

- Baby Belle (dwarf variety, suitable for growing in pots, miniature fruits).
- Black Beauty (pear shaped, open pollinated variety, upright foliage).
- Black Prince F1 (teardrop shaped fruit, very early, spineless).
- Moneymaker F1 (excellent, high yielding variety, glossy purple fruit).
- Rosa de Bianca (very attractive with pale pink and white skin. Average yield).
- Snow White (round, white fruit about 4cm in diameter, baby vegetable).

BASIL

Latin name: *Ocimum basilicum*
Family: *Labiatae*

Basil is such a wonderful crop for the polytunnel or greenhouse. It is a real sun and warmth lover and only thrives well with protection from the wind and rain. There is really nothing nicer than harvesting basil and using it in the kitchen either fresh, as pesto or even for flavouring oils.

SOIL AND SITE
Basil needs to be grown in full sun. It will not thrive if grown on the shady side of tall crops such as climbing beans or tomatoes. Some gardeners plant basil amongst their tomatoes as they require similar growing conditions, but, unfortunately, I have found this intercropping technique not very satisfactory as the basil usually suffers when the tomatoes are growing too tall and block out the light and rob all the nutrients from it.

Basil needs a reasonably fertile and free-draining soil. If the soil becomes waterlogged at any stage your plants will suffer and possibly succumb to aphid attack.

SOWING

Basil needs warmth to germinate so seeds should be sown in a warm room or even better on a heating bench. I usually make two sowings of basil: the first sowing in early April and the second in early June. I sow 4 seeds per cell about 1cm deep using organic seed compost. The seeds will germinate after about 10 days and are ready to plant out into the tunnel or greenhouse about 4–5 weeks after sowing. For an even higher quality crop you can pot the plants on into 9cm pots using a good potting compost. It is essential though that the pots remain on the heating bench or windowsill until they are ready for planting out.

SPACING
- Between plants: 20cm.
- Between rows: 30cm.

Note: do not separate the seedlings in the modules, plant all four together.

PLANT CARE

Watering basil properly is essential for producing a healthy crop. I think that most people generally water too much. A light watering twice a week should be sufficient. Obviously, if you notice that your plants are wilting you should water a little bit more.

HARVESTING

Many people do not know how to harvest basil properly. Instinctively people pick individual leaves and end up with a single tall bare stalk and a flowering shoot. To harvest basil properly you should wait until the plant is about 15cm tall and then remove the growing tips just above the second set of leaves, using a sharp knife or scissors. Just below the cut, two side-shoots will appear and when they are reasonably long you can cut them just above the first set of leaves. Then they will produce more side-shoots. As a result your plants will become bushier and grow healthier. Each plant can be harvested every 3–4 weeks so if you have 12 plants you can harvest 3 plants each week. The plants from the April sowing usually crop healthily until August. The June sowing will yield plenty of basil until October.

Fig. 2. *Correct harvesting of basil.*   Fig. 3. *After harvesting.*

POTENTIAL PROBLEMS

You will find that in some years basil grows very easily with no pest or disease problems at all. In other years it seems to be a major attraction for greenfly. As a prevention you could regularly spray a garlic/nettle tonic onto the plants. I usually spray every week from the time I plant them out until the plants are cleared.

HOW MUCH TO GROW?

If you only use a few leaves for occasional use in the kitchen two to three multi-sown plants are sufficient. If you are a more serious basil lover and make pesto and preserves you should have about 12 multi-sown plants which would cover only 1 square metre.

VARIETIES

There are well over one hundred varieties of basil. Some are well worth exploring for their curiosity. The best one for culinary use is the Sweet Basil, also called Sweet Genovese.

UNUSUAL TYPES
- Dark Opal (purple bronze foliage, 30cm high).
- Greek basil (compact plant with tiny leaves, 20cm high).
- Lemon basil (with a beautiful lemon fragrance).
- Purple Ruffles (with purple leaves, fringed and frilly, 30cm high).
- Thai basil (with mild anise flavour, attractive purple stems, 40cm high).

BEAN, CLIMBING FRENCH

Latin name: *Phaseolus vulgaris*
Family: *Leguminosae*

Climbing French beans are really a fantastic crop for a polytunnel or greenhouse. It is quite amazing how many beans you get from a small space indoors. Outdoors they only perform well in the warmer parts of the country or in more sheltered gardens. A tunnel is the ideal solution.

SOIL AND SITE
French beans require a very sunny and sheltered site. The soil should be fertile, moisture-retentive and free-draining. The soil pH can be slightly acidic ranging from 5.8–7.

As with any other tall crops be careful what you plant next to them as they will cause a lot of shade for plants growing behind them on the north side.

Vegetables such as lettuce, celery, dill and coriander may even benefit from some shade in mid summer whereas tomatoes, peppers, aubergines and basil will not crop well if there is any shade.

SOWING
Seeds can either be sown in pots for planting out later or sown directly into the ground. Two strategic sowings can produce beans from June until November.

FIRST SOWING
Sow 5 seeds into 9cm pots in the fourth week of March and place the pots on a heating bench or south-facing windowsill. The sowing depth is 5cm. In late April or early May plant each pot containing the five plants next to each cane of a climbing frame or preferably next to a string which is attached to an overhead wire and placed into the planting hole beneath the plants.

SECOND SOWING
The second sowing should be made in mid June for planting about 4 weeks later.

SPACING
A single row in the centre of the bed with strings 30cm apart in the row and 4–5 plants per station is ideal. The space on the edges of the beds can be used for quick maturing vegetables such as lettuce or annual spinach.

PLANT CARE
Regular watering is essential for good plant development and yield.

Fig. 4. Bean plants are trained up a string.

Watering should not be done from above as it may encourage fungal growth. The ideal time to water is in the morning so that there is less condensation on the plastic or glass at night.

Climbing French beans are allowed to climb up a string that is attached onto the overhead support wire. When the beans have reached the top of the climbing support, the growing tip should be nipped out.

HARVESTING

The beans are ready from June onwards until November. Once they crop they should be thoroughly picked at least once or twice a week. You should harvest the beans while they are still tender before the seeds begin to swell in the pods. The more they are picked, the more they will produce. Therefore, it is important to remove all the beans that have been overlooked during the previous harvest.

If the beans are left longer on the plants the majority of them will become tough and possibly stringy and the plants may stop flowering. Thus the yield will be dramatically reduced. So it is well worth letting your friends clear the crop when you are on holiday. Modern varieties are bred to be less stringy or completely stringless. I would recommend growing these varieties as it can be off-putting biting into a stringy bean.

As soon as the beans from the second sowing are starting to crop you could clear the first batch. Otherwise pests and diseases may spread onto the new crop.

STORING
French beans are best eaten fresh. If you have a glut of them, you can blanch and freeze them for the winter months.

POTENTIAL PROBLEMS
Slugs can be a big problem, especially when plants are young. Other pests include root aphids, black bean aphid and bean seed fly. Diseases include grey mould, foot and root rot, halo blight and viruses.

With good cultural practices (rotation, good healthy fertile soil, healthy seeds, resistant varieties) these problems can be overcome. A regular application of a garlic spray or seaweed may prevent many problems.

HOW MUCH TO GROW?
A single row about 1.5m long for each of the two sowings should provide plenty of beans for a family.

VARIETIES
- Blue Lake (pencil podded, very high yield).
- Cobra (high quality, tasty beans, available organically, resistant to bean mosaic virus).
- Eva (oval shaped pods, resistant to bean mosaic virus).

BEAN, DWARF FRENCH

Latin name: *Phaseolus vulgaris*
Family: *Leguminosae*

French beans are tender annuals, originating from Central and South America. There is great variation in pod types: green, yellow, purple or speckled. They may be flat, round, pencil shaped, long or short. The dwarf French beans grow to about 40cm with 25–30cm spread.

SOIL AND SITE
French beans require a very sunny and sheltered site. The soil should be fertile, moisture-retentive and free-draining. The soil pH can be slightly acidic ranging from 5.7–7.

SOWING
Seeds can either be sown indoors for planting out later, or sown directly into a well prepared seed bed.

FIRST SOWING

Sow 3 seeds into 7cm pots in the second week of March and place the pots on a heating bench or windowsill. The sowing depth is 3cm. They can be planted in the tunnel about 4 weeks later.

LAST SOWING

The last sowing can be made in mid to late June.

With these two sowings you can significantly prolong the cropping season of your French beans while still benefiting from your outdoor crop that is sown in May.

SPACING

- Between plants: 15cm.
- Between rows: 40cm.

HARVESTING

French beans can be harvested from June until the first frost. The pods should be picked regularly (once or twice a week), so they are still tender. If you do not harvest regularly the plant puts all its energy into ripening the seeds at the expense of new flowers and beans.

STORING

French beans are best eaten fresh. If you have a glut of them, you can blanch and freeze them for the winter months.

POTENTIAL PROBLEMS

Slugs can be a big problem, especially when plants are young. Other pests include root aphids, black bean aphid and bean seed fly. Diseases include grey mould, foot and root rot, halo blight and viruses. With good cultural practices (rotation, good healthy fertile soil, healthy seeds, resistant varieties) these problems can be overcome.

HOW MUCH TO GROW?
A 5m-long bed with a triple row of beans will yield about 10kg.

VARIETIES
- Cropper Teepee (green pods, excellent taste, pods are above the leaves).
- Purple Teepee (purple pods, excellent taste, pods are above the leaves).
- Safari (excellent modern variety, round pods, disease-resistant).
- Speedy (very early and high yielding, available as organic seed).
- Stanley (impressive yields of top quality beans, very early, disease-resistant).

BEAN, RUNNER

Latin name: *Phaseolus coccineus*
Family: *Leguminosae*

I wouldn't normally recommend growing runner beans under protection as they do quite well outdoors. However, if you love them you can extend their growing season by about two months at the beginning and end of the growing season in a tunnel. As they are very vigorous plants you should only plant them indoors if your tunnel or greenhouse is high enough.

SOIL AND SITE
Runner beans prefer a deep, rich, fertile soil with plenty of compost or composted manure dug in. Be careful what you plant next to the beans as they will cause a lot of shade on the north side for other

plants. Vegetables such as lettuce, celery, dill and coriander may even benefit from some shade in mid summer whereas tomatoes, peppers, aubergines and basil will not crop well if there is any shade.

SOWING

Seeds can either be sown in pots for planting out later or sown directly into the ground. Two strategic sowings will produce beans from June until November.

FIRST SOWING

Sow 5 seeds into 9cm pots in the third week of March and place the pots on a heating bench or south-facing windowsill. The sowing depth is 4cm. In late April plant each pot containing the five plants next to each cane of a climbing frame or preferably onto a string/twine which is attached to an overhead wire and placed into the planting hole beneath the plants.

SECOND SOWING

The second sowing can be made from mid to late June.

SPACING

A single row in the centre of the bed with strings 30cm apart in the row and 4–5 plants per station is ideal. It seems a waste of growing space to have just a single row per bed. In fact I used to plant them in a double row in the beds but unfortunately the disease pressure was too great and they suffered badly from fungal diseases from late summer onwards. The space on the edges of the beds can be used instead for quick maturing vegetables such as lettuce or annual spinach.

PLANT CARE

Regular watering is essential for good plant development and yield. I would recommend that watering should be done on the ground without getting the leaves wet especially from late summer onwards. The best time of day is mid morning. This is a precaution to lessen the danger of fungal attacks on your plants.

Research has found that the old fashioned practice of misting the flowers with water actually decreases the development of the pods.

TRAINING

Runner beans are climbers and need really sturdy climbing supports. The best and easiest way to train them in a tunnel is to tie a string onto the overhead support wire vertically and place the string into the planting hole planting the beans over it. The plants will then climb up. When the beans have reached the top of the climbing support, the growing tip should be nipped out.

Fig. 5. Runner beans planted onto string that is connected to overhead wire.

HARVESTING

The beans are ready from June onwards until November. Once they crop they should be thoroughly picked at least once or twice a week. You should harvest the beans while they are still tender before the seeds begin to swell in the pods. The more they are picked, the more they will produce. Therefore, it is important to remove all the beans that have been overlooked during the previous harvest.

If the beans are left longer on the plants the majority of them will become tough and possibly stringy and the plants may stop flowering. Thus the yield will be dramatically reduced. Modern varieties are bred to be less stringy or completely stringless.

As soon as the beans from the second sowing are ready you could clear the first batch.

POTENTIAL PROBLEMS
Grey mould (botrytis) is going to be your major problem especially during late summer when there is a lot of dense growth and a lack of air circulation in combination with cool, damp nights. It is essential to provide adequate ventilation and prune out infected leaves as much as possible.

HOW MUCH TO GROW?
A single row about 1.5m long for each of the two sowings should be sufficient for a family.

VARIETIES
- Achievement (produces masses of long, smooth and tender pods).
- Celebration (very early, most suited for early tunnel production, high yield).
- Enorma (my favourite variety, very large pods, very high yield, with good flavour).
- Lady Di (prolific cropper with an excellent nutty flavour).
- Scarlet Emperor (excellent flavour and texture, attractive red flowers).

BEETROOT

Latin name: *Beta vulgaris*
Family: *Chenopodiaceae* (Goosefoot Family)

Beetroot is a delicious and very easily grown vegetable. From just two outdoor sowings you can get a ten months' supply of roots. With the use of a tunnel or greenhouse you can get two extra months of supply in May and June. You need never be without beetroot again.

The best type for an early indoor sowing is the common red and round one. Keep the unusual varieties for outdoors. The most important consideration for an early sowing is that you have to choose a bolt-resistant variety. If you don't, a large percentage will go to seed prematurely and the roots will become inedible.

SOIL AND SITE

Beetroot prefers light, well-drained soil. Fresh manure application before sowing should be avoided. A dressing of old compost is very beneficial.

SOWING

It is important to remember that most beetroot seeds are clusters of more than one seed. This means if you sow one seed, you will have three to five seedlings germinating. These have to be thinned to one seedling soon after germination otherwise the beetroot will remain very small. Many modern varieties have single seeds. If you want to buy these you have to look out for monogerm varieties in seed catalogues.

Seeds can be sown directly in a well-prepared seed bed in shallow drills (1.5cm deep) from February until early April.

Some gardeners prefer to raise the seedlings in large modular trays. If you try this method make sure that you plant the seedlings out when they are still quite small. I always find beetroot very easy to sow directly as the seeds are large enough to handle and I do not want to clutter up valuable propagation space.

I initially sow the seeds about 2.5cm apart and then thin them in two stages. The first thinning is done a couple of weeks after germination. I remove all unwanted seedlings from the clusters (not for monogerm varieties) and leave one seedling every 5cm.

The thinnings rarely do well when transplanted. If you have gaps in the rows you are better off sowing a few new seeds.

When they reach the baby beetroot stage you can harvest every second plant. These are delicious and you can also cook the leaves like spinach. This allows the remaining plants to develop fully.

If you want to grow large beetroot you can increase the spacing to 15cm between plants.

SPACING
- Between plants: 10cm.
- Between rows: 25cm.

PLANT CARE
Apart from keeping the crop weed-free and properly thinned to the required spacing, there is no other maintenance required.

HARVESTING

Early beetroot from a February or March sowing can be harvested in May. The April sown crop can be harvested in June. Early beetroot will not store well. If you have a glut or if you need to make space in your tunnel or greenhouse, you could harvest the roots. Twist off the leaves and put them in a plastic bag in the fridge. They should keep for about a month.

POTENTIAL PROBLEMS

Beetroot is a very healthy vegetable. There is no specific pest or disease that affects it. Slugs may eat young seedlings especially if sown too early or if the garden is a bit wild but generally they go for the other vegetables first.

Beetroot is very sensitive to a deficiency of boron in the soil. The symptoms are brown sunken patches on the roots and black areas inside the root. A soil test prior to sowing could identify the problem.

VARIETIES

- For the early sowings in February and March you have to choose bolt-resistant varieties.
- My favourite variety of beetroot is 'Pablo F1'. I have grown it for the last few years and I have given up experimenting with other varieties because this one is just perfect. In case you cannot get 'Pablo F1' you can try:
- Boltardy (bolt-resistant, very early variety).
- Bikores (bolt-resistant, round oval shaped, deep red internal colouring).
- Bulls Blood (a dual purpose variety with blood red edible leaves and roots).
- Detroit Globe (an old heritage variety with excellent taste).
- Jannis (an improved selection of Boltardy).
- For the April sowing under protection you can choose any of your favourite varieties.

CABBAGE

Latin name: *Brassica oleracea* (Capitata Group)
Family: *Brassicaceae* (also known as *Cruciferae*)

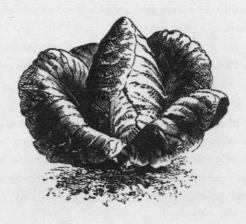

Cabbages are the most commonly grown member of the brassica family. They generally do extremely well in our cool, moist climate provided that plenty of compost or ripened manure is available. Thus they are not really suitable for growing under protection as they dislike extreme heat during the summer. The only time I grow them in a tunnel or greenhouse is in later winter/early spring.

SOIL AND SITE
Cabbages are greedy plants and so require a high level of soil fertility. Composted manure should be incorporated a few weeks prior to planting.

The pH level of the soil should be above 6.5, otherwise it should be corrected either in the form of calcified seaweed or ground limestone. An acid soil may encourage the spread of clubroot.

SOWING

I prefer sowing cabbages in modular seed trays which are placed on a heating bench in a greenhouse or on a warm windowsill. I sow one or two seeds per module about 1.5cm deep. If two seeds germinate you have to remove the weaker seedling. They usually germinate within 5–7 days and are ready for planting out about 5 weeks after sowing.

The first sowing can be done as early as late January. A second sowing can be made in late February for planting in late March.

SPACING

The spacing of the plants determines the final size of the head. If lots of small cabbages are required plant them closer.

I usually space the plants 25 x 25cm apart. As soon as the growing plants touch each other I harvest every second plant as spring greens (non-hearted leafy cabbage) and to give the remaining plants space to bulk up.

PLANT CARE

Cabbages require a firm soil. The transplants should be well watered before transplanting. They should be planted firmly with a trowel or dibber. Regular hoeing will control weed growth whilst stimulating plant vigour.

HARVESTING

Spring greens can be harvested from early April onwards. The first headed spring cabbages are ready from late April until early June. Be aware though that these early cabbages have hardly any shelf life. As soon as they are ready they are prone to crack open. So it's essential to harvest and eat them as soon as they have filled out.

POTENTIAL PROBLEMS

Cabbages are susceptible to the same insect and disease pests as all the other brassicas but due to the early cropping period most problems will be avoided.

VARIETIES

- Hispi F1 (pointed cabbage suitable for spring and summer use).
- Pyramid F1 (dark green pointed variety).

CALABRESE

Latin name: *Brassica oleracea* (Italica Group)
Family: *Brassicaceae* (also known as *Cruciferae*)

What consumers call broccoli, gardeners call calabrese. So if you want to grow the broccoli from the shops you have to buy calabrese seeds. Throughout most of the year calabrese will grow better outside but there is the possibility to extend the cropping season both in spring and autumn with the use of a tunnel or greenhouse.

SOIL AND SITE

Calabrese requires a sunny unshaded place in the tunnel or greenhouse. The soil should be fertile, free-draining but with a high water-holding capacity. The soil should preferably have been enriched with plenty of well-rotted farmyard manure.

SOWING

For tunnel or greenhouse production, calabrese is best sown in late January to early March and again in early July until early August. I always sow calabrese in modular trays which are placed in a greenhouse. I sow one or two seeds per module about 1.5cm deep. If two seeds germinate you have to remove the weaker seedling. They usually germinate within 5–7 days and are ready for planting out about 4 weeks after sowing. For continuity I would sow a few seeds at regular intervals.

SPACING

For tunnel production the ideal spacing for calabrese is 30cm x 60cm. With this spacing a good yield of average sized heads as well as numerous side-shoots are produced over a period of approximately a month, provided the soil fertility is high.

PLANT CARE

Calabrese requires plenty of water at all stages. Drying out results in smaller plants and premature budding so the heads remain small.

HARVESTING

Cropping from the early sowing will probably start in late April/early May. The later sowings will produce right up to the first hard frost.

The central head should be cut before the flowers open. Smaller side-shoots will develop later and one can expect 2–3 further cuts.

Generally cropping may start about 70–100 days after sowing depending on the variety and season.

STORING

Calabrese is best eaten fresh. However, if you have a glut the heads can be blanched and frozen.

POTENTIAL PROBLEMS

Calabrese is susceptible to the same pests and diseases as cabbage and the same control measures are recommended. The main problem with calabrese is premature flowering. It is crucial to check your plants for ripeness at least twice a week as the buds quickly open up into yellow flowers and become useless.

VARIETIES

- Belstar F1 (a vigorous large-headed variety).
- Green Magic F1 (very early variety, producing attractive dome-shaped heads, good disease-resistance).
- Fiesta F1 (reliable variety, good taste, well suited for later sowings).
- Kabuki F1 (matures in 70 days, very early, small plant, ideal for baby head production, mildew-resistant).
- Marathon F1 (mid season variety, blue green heads, good disease and cold resistance).
- Tiara F1 (very early variety, good flavour).

CAPE GOOSEBERRY

Latin name: *Physalis peruviana*
Family: *Solanaceae*

The fruits of the cape gooseberry are often referred to as Chinese Lantern. They are delicious with a sweet and tangy flavour.

The cape gooseberry originated in Peru (thus the Latin name: *peruviana*) and naturalized in South Africa (the Cape). From there it moved to northern Europe in the nineteenth century.

SOIL AND SITE

The cape gooseberry requires a place in full sun and a reasonably fertile soil. Avoid the use of fresh manure otherwise your plants will grow too tall and spindly. Well balanced nutrition with very old compost is more appropriate.

SOWING

Cape gooseberries should be sown in early April on a heating bench (20°C) or south-facing windowsill. I usually broadcast (sprinkle) a few tiny seeds into a 9cm pot containing a good seed compost and only cover the seeds very lightly. When the first true leaves appear

I prick the seedlings out into individual small (7cm) pots using a potting compost. The pots should remain on the heating bench. The plants can be planted out into the polytunnel or greenhouse in May when the danger of frost has passed.

SPACING
The plants are large and have a habit of sprawling so they require a lot of space.
• Between plants: 1.2 metres.

PLANT CARE
Apart from regular watering there is very little else to do. You may occasionally place a few plant supports around the plants to prevent them from sprawling.

HARVESTING
Only in the warmer parts of the country will you get a reliable harvest of Chinese Lanterns. In the cooler parts you will be hoping for a warm summer. They are ready when the outside papery husks turn brown and the fruit inside turns golden orange.

POTENTIAL PROBLEMS
The greenhouse whitefly can become a nuisance with this crop. The control methods are the same as for tomatoes.

HOW MUCH TO GROW?
One or two plants are quite sufficient as they take up a lot of room and are not always reliable croppers.

VARIETIES
• Dwarf Gold (a compact variety with golden orange fruits in neat husks) can be grown in containers.

CARROT

Latin name: *Daucus carota* var. *sativus*
Family: *Umbelliferae* (also known as *Apiaceae*)

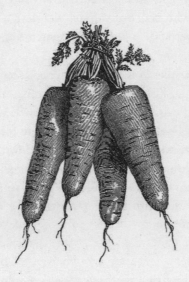

Gardeners wouldn't usually consider growing carrots in a tunnel or greenhouse. But if you choose a suitable variety and sow them very early in the year you will get fantastic carrots from May until July when there are few carrots around. In fact late winter/early spring is the only time I would grow carrots indoors. The other major advantage is that you won't get the carrot root fly.

TYPES OF CARROTS
Not all types and varieties are suitable for early carrot production under protection. The suitable varieties for early indoor production are often referred to as 'forcing' types or 'first earlies'. Forcing means that the plants can be forced to grow at such an early time. Other

varieties (non-forcing types) will be a lot more likely to bolt and run to seed prematurely.

SOIL AND SITE

Carrots do best on light and stone-free soil which is free-draining. I know gardeners who take out the soil and sieve it before they sow their carrots. I have never gone to that extreme and have no plans for it in the future. The ideal soil pH is 5.8–7.

Always remember that you should never add fresh manure to the soil before sowing. This applies even more to carrot production indoors as this will cause too much leafy growth at the expense of root development. The roots would also tend to fork, trying to find the pockets of manure, rather than growing down. Forking of the roots also occurs if there are stones in the ground.

Only if the soil has a poor structure, very well-rotted compost can be dug into it in the autumn. Ensure that the compost is well blended in with the soil.

SOWING

Carrots require a very fine seed bed. Seeds should be sown about 2cm deep in shallow drills and thinned to the required spacing. Weed control is essential in the early stages of growth to get the plants established.

The first sowing can be made as early as November, but I prefer to wait until late January. The beds can be pre-warmed by placing a sheet of black plastic onto the beds for a few weeks before the carrots are sown. Remove the plastic before the carrots are sown. After sowing you could place a fleece over the growing crop to protect it from the cold. While both of these covers help the carrot crop they are not essential, they merely speed up the crop.

I often make a second sowing in March which will provide carrots until July.

SPACING
- Between plants: 3–5cm.
- Between rows: 20–25cm.

PLANT CARE
Carrots should be kept well weeded at all times because they are bad competitors with weeds. The soil should always be kept moist in the early stages. When the plants are established you can water once or twice a week, depending how warm it is.

Irregular watering causes splitting of the roots. There is no requirement for any additional feed throughout the growing season. You really want the roots to grow down in search of food.

HARVESTING
Early carrots can be pulled and bunched as required. On heavier soil it is recommended to fork the roots out as they may otherwise break. The harvesting season is from May until July.

STORAGE
Early carrots do not store well so you should only harvest when required. Many people think that carrots keep better if the leaves are still attached. However, quite the opposite is true. The leaves pull out the moisture from the roots and they quickly shrivel. If you want to store early carrots for a few weeks you should twist off the leaves as you harvest them and store the roots in a plastic bag in the fridge.

POTENTIAL PROBLEMS
There are fewer problems with indoor carrots. The dreaded carrot root fly is rarely a problem with the early sowings. You can prevent the root fly from entering the tunnel by covering up the lower part of the door with a frame covered with Bionet or plastic. It should be one metre high.

Other problems you may encounter with an early sowing are poor germination, forked roots, split roots, bolting and too much leaf growth and not a lot of roots.

Poor germination can occur if the soil temperature is too low. Check the temperature with a soil thermometer and only sow when the temperature is above 7°C. Pre–warm the beds if necessary with black plastic.

Other reasons for poor germination could be poor quality or old seed and the possibility of the seed bed drying out.

You may get forked or misshaped roots if the carrots are in contact with fresh manure, if the soil is stony or compacted. Overcrowding causes roots to curl around each other. To prevent such problems you should dig deeply to break the compacted layers and remove any larger stones and thin your plants early to the recommended spacing. I often find that some varieties have a much lower percentage of misshaped roots. The variety Rocket F1 seems to suffer a lot less from it. This variety also gets no green shoulder like many others do when the neck is exposed to light.

Bolting can be a serious problem with early sowings but only if you choose the wrong variety. Carrots are biennial plants. This means that they fulfil their lifecycle from seed to seed in two years. The winter cold and the warming up in spring will let them know that they are in their second year and should be flowering and producing seed. Sometimes they get confused especially in a tunnel or greenhouse. You may suddenly get a warm spell in February (it can get quite hot when the sun shines on the glass or plastic) followed by a very cold spell in March and warming up again in April. So within three months the plants thought it was autumn, winter and spring. And then they bolt. When plants bolt they absorb all the stored food from all plant parts especially from the tap root and use it for flower and seed production and the carrots will become as tough as old boots. The varieties listed opposite are less likely to bolt.

HOW MUCH TO GROW?

You will get about 100 small to medium sized carrots in one square metre. If you eat 2 bunches of carrots (8 carrots/bunch) per week from mid May until mid July (8 weeks) you will need 130 carrots. One and a half square metres is sufficient for that requirement.

VARIETIES

- Amsterdam Forcing (first early).
- Buror F1 (first early, excellent for growing under cover).
- Napoli F1 (very early, slightly tapered roots).
- Rocket F1 (early, excellent flavour and no green shoulder).
- Namur F1 (suitable for early indoor production, Nantes type).

CAULIFLOWER, MINI

Latin name: *Brassica oleracea* (Botrytis Group)
Family: *Brassicaceae* (also known as *Cruciferae*)

You may have never considered growing cauliflowers in a tunnel or greenhouse because they take up valuable growing space and actually do quite well or even better outdoors. The only reason to grow them indoors is for the production of mini-cauliflowers. All mini vegetables are in fashion as they are very handy for small families and individuals.

SOIL AND SITE
Cauliflowers require a fertile, deep soil. The ideal pH is 6.5–7.0. Acid soils can lock up essential trace elements and this may cause defects such as whiptail and tipburn.

Cauliflowers prefer cool growing conditions. A temperature of 16–18°C combined with a moderately high humidity is ideal. So early spring and autumn is the best time to grow mini-cauliflowers indoors.

SOWING

I generally sow cauliflowers in modular trays which are placed on a heating bench (18°C) in a greenhouse. The alternative is a south-facing windowsill in the house. I sow one or two seeds per module about 1.5cm deep. If two seeds germinate you have to remove the weaker seedling. They usually germinate within 5–7 days and are ready for planting out about 4 weeks after sowing.

For tunnel and greenhouse production sow from late January until early April and again from mid June until late July.

SPACING

A spacing of 20 x 20cm will produce small curds about 10cm in diameter. The spacing can be adjusted either way to get different sized curds. For example, a spacing of 15 x 15cm will produce curds of 6cm in diameter and a spacing of 25 x 25cm will produce 12cm curds.

PLANT CARE

The soil should be kept moist at all times. Good ventilation is essential to prevent fungal diseases.

HARVESTING

If the cauliflowers are not harvested on time the curds will turn brown and rot.

When harvesting cauliflowers you should keep their leaf wrapping intact to protect the curd from damage.

POTENTIAL PROBLEMS

Cauliflowers are susceptible to the same pests and diseases as cabbage and the same control measures are recommended.

Cauliflowers may also encounter other problems such as whiptail and tipburn. Whiptail can be a problem on acidic soil where molybdenum is made unavailable to plants. The plants develop chlorosis (yellowing) between the leaf veins and in severe cases they may develop 'blind growth' (absence of growing point). Once the damage is seen it is too late to rescue the crop but liming the soil will help in future years.

Tipburn may also be a problem on acidic soils. The symptoms are brown margins on younger leaves and a discoloration of the curds. This is caused by calcium deficiency.

HOW MUCH TO GROW?

For mini-cauliflowers at a spacing of 20 x 20cm you'll get 20 mini-cauliflowers per square metre.

VARIETIES

Suitable varieties:

- Freedom F1 (excellent new variety, can be grown as standard or as mini-cauliflower).
- Igloo (excellent variety, suitable for mini-cauliflower production).
- Mayflower F1 (excellent for the earliest sowings in January and February).
- Rafale F1 (compact variety with uniform pure white curds).

CELERY

Latin name: *Apium graveolens L.* var. *dulce*
Family: *Umbelliferae* (also known as *Apiaceae*)

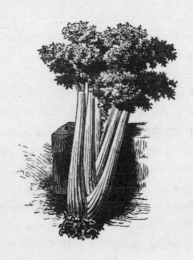

I often find celery difficult to grow outdoors. The stems can become quite tough and dry. In a tunnel or greenhouse, however, we can all grow fantastic celery far sweeter, crunchier and juicier than from any shop. Even people who claim not to like celery will change their mind after tasting home grown celery from a tunnel or greenhouse.

The secret of growing good celery is to choose a good variety and grow it on a fertile soil with plenty of moisture.

The older types of celery required blanching of the stems in order to rid it of its unpleasantly strong flavour and green colour. This process involved digging a trench and planting the celery inside and gradually filling up the trench as the celery grew. I have never come across anyone who grows celery in this way nowadays.

Over the last few decades many self-blanching varieties have appeared and made it much easier to grow celery. No trenching or blanching is required.

SOIL AND SITE
Celery prefers a rich, loamy soil with plenty of well-rotted compost added to it. The pH should be between 6.5 and 7.0. It can even grow in a more shady part of the tunnel (behind climbing beans or tomatoes) provided there is adequate ventilation.

SOWING
I usually broadcast (sprinkle) the tiny seeds into a standard seed tray or pot containing seed compost. It is very important not to cover the seeds as they require light to germinate. The pots or trays should be placed on a heating bench or on a warm south-facing windowsill. The seeds take about 2 weeks to germinate. The seedlings can be pricked out into modular trays when they are 3cm tall (about 2 weeks after germination). It is important that they are pricked out at an early stage otherwise there will be too much root disturbance which may lead to bolting at a later stage. It takes about 8–10 weeks from sowing to planting out.

For continuity you can sow every 3 weeks from late February until early June. All sowings can be planted in the tunnel or greenhouse.

SPACING
The highest yields can be achieved by a spacing of 27 x 27cm each way. If you want smaller plants you can decrease the distance to 20 x 20cm or if you want to show off increase it to 35 x 35cm.

PLANT CARE
Celery in its natural state is a wetland plant so it requires a consistent water supply. If drip irrigation is used I would still

recommend some additional overhead watering with a watering can. Lack of water will make the stalks fibrous and bitter. If the plants look stunted you could sprinkle some organic poultry pellets around them to provide the plants with a quick boost of energy.

HARVESTING
Celery can be harvested about 10 weeks after planting. It will last well for about 3 weeks and then becomes fibrous and tough.

Harvest the whole plant when the stalks are reasonably big and before they get stringy. If you want to keep it for a few days harvest early in the morning and trim the tips of the leaves to leave about 25cm of stem and keep in a plastic bag in the fridge. They should keep for a month. The cut off leaves can be used immediately in soups or as a flavouring.

POTENTIAL PROBLEMS
Tunnel grown celery generally grows very healthily. Even the carrot root fly seems to leave it alone indoors. The celery leaf miner (also known as the celery fly) may sometimes cause damage. Tiny maggots tunnel within the leaves and cause irregular shaped blisters.

HOW MUCH TO GROW?
You will get 12 plants per square metre. Once mature, celery will only stand for 3 weeks in the garden, so only grow a few at a time.

VARIETIES
- Celebrity (early maturing with crisp, nutty flavoured stems).
- Lathom Blanching Galaxy (an excellent well flavoured and reliable variety).
- Victoria F1 (excellent variety, great flavour, green colour and long standing ability).

CHERVIL

Latin name: *Anthriscus cerefolium*
Family: *Umbelliferae* (also known as *Apiaceae*)

Chervil is not yet a popular herb, but I include it in this book because I think it's one of the underrated cut herbs. With its refreshing flavour it is an ideal ingredient for any salad. Chervil has never been developed by plant breeders so there are very few named varieties available. Like dill and coriander it is a very short lived annual and thus needs to be sown at regular intervals.

SOIL AND SITE
Chervil will grow on any reasonably fertile soil. A small compost application prior to planting is sufficient. During the summer months it can be grown in part shade.

SOWING
For continuity you can sow every three weeks from mid February until early September. The early sowings (February to late April) and late sowings (August to September) should be planted in a

tunnel or greenhouse whereas the other sowings can be planted outdoors.

The early sowings require some additional heat ideally from a heating bench. I generally sow chervil in modular trays (5–7 seeds per cell) and they are ready for planting about 4 weeks later.

SPACING
- Between rows: 25cm
- Between plants: 15cm (groups of 5 to 7 plants)

PLANT CARE
Apart from regular weeding and watering there is little else to do. Good tunnel or greenhouse ventilation is essential.

HARVESTING
With successional sowings you can expect to harvest chervil nearly all year round. You can either pick individual leaves if only small quantities are required or use the cut-and-come-again technique.

Cut when the plants are about 15cm tall. You can expect to get two to three cuts per plant. As soon as the new batch is producing well it is best to discard the older ones.

POTENTIAL PROBLEMS
I have never encountered any problems with chervil.

HOW MUCH TO GROW
Two to three multi-seeded plants sown every three weeks will be adequate.

VARIETIES
- Massa (an excellent new variety with dark green, smooth leaves).

CHICORY

Latin name: *Cichorium intybus*
Family: *Compositae* (also known as *Asteraceae*)

Apart from the red radicchio which we get in many restaurants and often leave on the side, chicory in all its forms and types is still quite uncommon. This is due to its bitter taste which takes a while to get used to. On the positive side some types of chicory are very easy to grow and more or less free from pests and diseases.

There are three types of chicory and two of them are well suited to tunnel or greenhouse production – the forcing chicory and radicchio. The third type – Sugarloaf or Pan di Zucchero – grows better outside.

Forcing chicory

The forcing or blanching of chicory originated in Belgium (1840) and the Belgians are still the masters of producing this delicious vegetable. To produce the 'chicons' (the name of the heads) you sow a 'Witloof' chicory variety in May outdoors. The long tap roots should be carefully dug out from October until December. They look a bit like dandelion roots. The leaves should then be trimmed off about 2.5cm above the root.

The roots can be stored in boxes of sand in a cold place until they are required for forcing. To force them, simply replant a few roots at a time in the tunnel or greenhouse soil with their necks just above the soil. After watering, cover the bed with thick black plastic. After about 4–6 weeks the small heads (chicons) are ready to harvest. Regular planting of the taproots will provide you with a wonderful supply of winter salad.

Radicchio

Radicchio is a very attractive salad that is very popular in Italy. It is frequently used in restaurants as decoration. The leaves turn increasingly red as the temperature decreases. There are now excellent varieties available that are suitable for a tunnel or greenhouse.

SOIL AND SITE

Almost any fertile soil will produce good chicory. Apply well decomposed compost.

SOWING

Forcing or Witloof chicory

Sow thinly in drills 30cm apart. Thin the plants to about 20cm apart in the row. Alternatively the seeds can be raised in modular trays (1–2 seeds per cell and thinned out to leave just one seedling) then planted out about 4–5 weeks later. If they are raised in modular trays it is essential that the seedlings are planted out at a young development stage otherwise the taproot may become 'air-pruned' and start to fork at a later stage.

Radicchio

Radicchio can be sown in modular trays from late June until early August for planting in a tunnel or greenhouse. It does not tend to germinate as easily as lettuce so I usually sow two seeds in each module and thin to just one plant per module.

The seeds should be sown 1cm deep at a temperature of 15–18°C and planted out at a spacing of 30 x 30cm about 4–5 weeks after sowing.

To get a regular supply, sow only small amounts at fortnightly intervals.

PLANT CARE
Keep the plants well watered.

HARVESTING AND STORING
The tap roots of the forcing 'Witloof' types should be dug out in October and placed in a box with alternate layers of sand and roots and forced as required throughout the winter. Once ready the chicons (heads) will last for about a week in a plastic bag in the fridge.

The red radicchio types should be sown in succession as they do not keep well once harvested. It is best to harvest early in the morning, ideally at dawn.

POTENTIAL PROBLEMS
The only problems I have ever encountered with chicory are slugs and grey mould (botrytis) during wet weather.

HOW MUCH TO GROW?
Just grow a few to see how you like them.

VARIETIES

Witloof chicory

- Brussels Witloof (one of the best known forcing types).
- Zoom F1 (high quality chicons, easy to force).

Radicchio

- Cesare (an Italian variety for autumn harvest, very colourful).
- Palla Rossa (delicate flavour, colour turns red when it gets colder).
- Rossa di Treviso (crisp green leaves which turn red when cold).

CHILLI PEPPER

Latin name: *Capsicum frutescens annuum*
Family: *Solanaceae*

INTRODUCTION

When Christopher Columbus discovered America he believed that he found the black pepper (native of Asia) but in fact it was only the chilli pepper with its fiery taste.

Chilli peppers are a wonderful crop for a polytunnel or greenhouse. They are a lot easier to grow than peppers and their yield can be phenomenal. In some years I harvested around 100 chillies per plant and we had six plants!

Beware, though, as some varieties are extremely spicy. The Scoville test rates the heat of chillies on a scale of zero to over a million Scoville Heat Units (SHU). The world's hottest chilli is the

Naga Jolokia. Chilli enthusiasts always try to breed an even hotter chilli. Always be careful when handling chillies!

SOIL AND SITE
Chilli peppers prefer a rich, loamy soil with plenty of well-rotted compost added to it. The pH should be between 6.5 and 7.0. They need to grow in full sun so ensure that there is no shading from other crops.

SOWING
Chilli peppers require a long growing season and should be sown as early as February until mid March at the latest. I usually sow the seeds in a small standard seed tray or pot and space the seeds 2cm apart from each other covered with 1cm compost. The tray should be placed into a warm propagator or warm windowsill. The temperature should be around 18–21°C. The seedlings start to appear 2 weeks after sowing. About 10 days after they have germinated they should be pricked out into 7cm pots using potting compost. Three or four weeks later they can be potted on into a 10cm pot.

PLANTING
Chilli peppers dislike cold temperatures so they can only be planted into the greenhouse or tunnel in early May in mild areas or in mid to late May in cooler districts.

SPACING
- Between plants: 45cm.
- Between rows: 45cm.

PLANT CARE
Apart from regular watering there is little else you need to do. If the plants grow too upright you can pinch out the growing shoot at

about 30cm height. This encourages the plants to become bushier. Depending on the variety this may not be necessary as some branch out naturally. The plants usually require a single stake to prevent them from falling over.

HARVESTING AND STORING

Harvest chillies throughout the summer whenever required. All chillies start off green and then turn into their final colour which nearly encompasses the whole colour spectrum. Green chillies are a little less hot. Towards the end of the growing season in October I usually harvest all the remaining chillies and dry them in the kitchen. The children make them into "necklaces" that can be hung in the kitchen. They will last for well over a year.

POTENTIAL PROBLEMS

Chilli peppers are very prone to aphid attacks. Both whitefly and greenfly feed on the leaves of the plants. A regular application of a garlic spray before the problem arises can provide an effective control. If aphids are already present a biological control can be used.

HOW MUCH TO GROW?

Three plants are usually sufficient for a year round supply of chillies.

VARIETIES

- Demon Red (very decorative with compact habit, suitable for pots. ripens from green to red, very hot).
- Hungarian Hot Wax (not a hot chilli at all, tastes more like a pepper, but very prolific).
- Naga Jolokia (the world's hottest chilli, measured over one million Scoville Heat Units, use sparingly!).

- Navaho (an early and high yielding semi-hot chilli. Small conical shaped fruits, 10cm long).
- Prairie Fire (one of my favourite varieties, produces over a hundred hot and well flavoured small chillies).
- Purple Tiger (compact habit, can be grown in pots, small purple fruits and tri-coloured foliage).
- Ring O'Fire (extremely hot chillies on small plants).

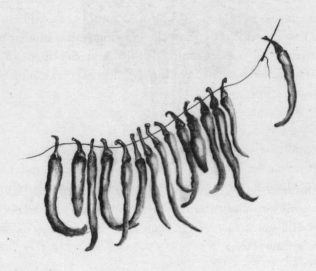

Fig. 6. Chilli necklace.

CHINESE CABBAGE

Latin name: *Brassica rapa* (Pekinensis Group)
Family: *Brassicaceae* (also known as *Cruciferae*)

Chinese cabbage has become very popular in continental Europe, both for gardeners and consumers. It is a delicious vegetable and very easy and quick to grow. It is an ideal late season crop for a tunnel or greenhouse.

TYPES
There are three types of Chinese cabbage:
Cylindrical type
It has long erect leaves which form a cylindrical head.
Barrel headed type
It has a compact barrel shaped dense head.
Loose headed type
It produces leaves without forming a head.

The barrel headed types are the most common and popular ones.

SOIL AND SITE

Chinese cabbage requires a deep, fertile and well-drained soil with good water retention and a pH range of 5.5–7. A generous application of well decomposed compost or manure is essential.

SOWING

Chinese cabbage is an excellent crop for late summer. Earlier sowings are usually less successful as the plants are more likely to bolt and are more prone to fleabeetle attacks. I generally sow one seed per cell into a modular tray. The plants are ready to transplant 3–4 weeks after sowing. For a regular supply sow every 2 weeks from early June until August.

SPACING

The plants should be spaced 45 x 45cm apart.

PLANT CARE

Chinese cabbage has a very shallow root system and it requires unchecked, rapid growth. To achieve this you need to water regularly to keep the soil moist at all times. If the growth is stunted you can sprinkle a small amount of organic poultry pellets around the plants. This will provide the plants with a quick boost of energy.

HARVESTING

Harvest the mature heads when they are firm. The heads will keep for a few weeks if placed in a plastic bag in the fridge.

POTENTIAL PROBLEMS

Chinese cabbage may suffer from the usual brassica pests and diseases. Fleabeetles are a particular problem with them. If there is a fleabeetle problem on nearby crops it is best to cover the Chinese cabbages as soon as they are planted securely with fleece. If it's well covered the fleabeetles can't get to it.

HOW MUCH TO GROW?
You will get 8–10 heads per square metre.

VARIETIES
- Yuki F1 (my favourite variety, oval heads and slow to bolt).
- Kasumi F1 (fast growing variety with oval head, slow to bolt).

CLAYTONIA

Latin name: *Montia perfoliata*
Family: *Portulacaceae*

Claytonia is often called winter purslane and sometimes miner's lettuce. It got the name miner's lettuce because of its use as a fresh salad green by miners in the 1849 Gold Rush in California.

It is one of these amazingly productive salad plants that will keep you in fresh healthy greens throughout the winter. It is also a favourite of small children who wouldn't touch other salads. It is an ideal crop for the polytunnel and greenhouse as it makes excellent use of the space when not much else can grow.

SOIL AND SITE
In its native North America it grows in acid sandy soils but it can cope easily with a wide range of soil and site conditions. It prefers cool damp growing conditions.

SOWING

The best – and possibly the only – time to sow claytonia is in late August to late September. You will get well-established transplants ready to plant in October for harvesting from November until April the following year. There is not much point in sowing it at any other time as it will bolt prematurely.

I usually sow a pinch of seeds in modules (5–7 seeds per cell). The modules are ready for planting about 5 weeks after sowing.

SPACING
- Between rows: 25cm.
- Between plants: 20cm (5–7 plants per station).

PLANT CARE

It is essential to keep the plot completely weed-free and watered regularly.

HARVESTING

You can either harvest individual leaves as they are needed or use the cut-and-come again method: cut the whole plant at about 5cm height from the soil level and the leaves will re-grow within the next 2–3 weeks. After cutting it you should tidy up the plant and remove any old or decaying stalks.

Claytonia can be eaten fresh as a salad or it can be boiled like spinach. It is a wonderful cropper and often you will have a surplus that you can make into a delicious fresh winter soup.

POTENTIAL PROBLEMS

Apart from slugs and snails there are no pests and diseases that affect claytonia. It certainly is one of the easiest salads you can possibly grow.

VARIETIES

There are no named varieties of claytonia.

Claytonia is somewhat of a botanical curiosity. The flowers are grouped together above a pair of leaves that are united together around the stem and appear as one circular leaf.

CORIANDER

Latin name: *Coriandrum sativum*
Family: *Umbelliferae* (also known as *Apiaceae*)

After parsley and basil, coriander is the third bestselling herb. There are so many dishes where coriander is an essential ingredient. It is also such an amazingly fast and easy herb to grow. If you sow a small amount at regular intervals you can get coriander for ten months of the year. Make sure you purchase seeds from a variety that is suitable for leaf production. Normal coriander seed (without a variety name) is better for seed production.

SOIL AND SITE
Coriander is such an easy plant to grow. Any reasonably fertile soil will do. It can even be grown in semi-shade.

SOWING

For continuity you can sow every 2–3 weeks from early February until mid September. The early sowings (February to late April) and late sowings (August to September) should be planted in a tunnel or greenhouse whereas the other sowings can be planted outdoors.

The very early sowings in February and March should be done in modular trays and placed on a heating bench at 18°C. I generally sow a small pinch of seeds (about 5–7) per cell. The seedlings are not divided when planted out about 4 weeks later.

When the soil has warmed sufficiently, seeds can be sown directly into a well prepared seed bed.

Whichever method you use it is vital that the seed compost or seed bed does not dry out at any stage. If your seedlings suffer in the trays from a lack of water they start to panic and run into seed before they are even planted out. They also react like this if they are left for too long in the modules. You have to be careful that you plant the modules out before the plants get pot-bound. This is about 3–4 weeks after sowing.

SPACING
- Between rows: 25cm.
- Between plants: 15cm (groups of 5–7 plants).

PLANT CARE

It is important to keep coriander growing steadily otherwise it is very prone to bolting. This can be achieved by keeping the soil moist and the tunnel or greenhouse well ventilated.

HARVESTING

With successional sowings you can expect to harvest coriander from late March until November. You can pick individual leaves if only small quantities are required.

Alternatively you can use the cut-and-come-again technique. When the plant is about 15cm tall you can cut the whole plant at about 5cm height from soil level. The leaves will regrow within a few weeks and you can repeat the cutting.

You can expect to get two to three good cuts per plant. As soon as the new batch is producing well it is best to discard the older ones.

POTENTIAL PROBLEMS
Coriander is such a short-lived crop that very little can bother it. If it is well grown and not left for too long in the ground you should have no problem with it.

HOW MUCH TO GROW?
You will get 24 plants (groups of 5–7) per square metre. Each group may yield up to 30g. Sowing 5 cells every 2–3 weeks should be adequate for a family's needs.

VARIETIES
- Calypso (a new variety, extremely slow to bolt).
- Leisure (large leaves, specially produced for leaf production, ideal for later sowings).
- Santos (excellent for leaf production for early sowings).
- Slobolt (good all rounder).

CORN SALAD

Latin name: *Valerianella locusta*
Family: *Valerianaceae*

Corn salad grows wild in many parts of Europe and is often considered a weed in cultivated land. It is also known as lamb's lettuce. The small leaves have a wonderful nutty flavour and the plants are completely winter hardy. It makes an excellent winter crop for your polytunnel or greenhouse. Compared to other winter salads it is quite low yielding and is not suitable for the cut-and-come-again system but is still well worth growing as it is one of the healthiest salads you can grow. It contains three times as much vitamin C and beta-carotene as lettuce.

You usually harvest the whole plant.

SOIL AND SITE
Corn salad will grow in any reasonably fertile soil. It is completely undemanding.

SOWING
Corn salad is best sown towards the end of the year. You can sow the seeds directly into your polytunnel or greenhouse (1cm deep)

at fortnightly intervals from the end of August until early October. Spring and summer sowings are less reliable as they run to seed prematurely.

SPACING
- Between rows: 15cm.
- Between plants: 7cm.

PLANT CARE
It is essential to keep the plot completely weed-free. The soil should be kept moist throughout the growing period.

HARVESTING
The whole plant should be harvested when about 10–15cm in diameter. The plants can be harvested from October until March. After that they will start to bolt.

POTENTIAL PROBLEMS
Apart from slugs and snails there are no pests that affect corn salad. Mildew, however, can become a serious problem if your greenhouse is not well ventilated.

HOW MUCH TO GROW?
Two square metres of corn salad (sown at intervals) will provide you with healthy greens for many winter salads.

VARIETIES
- Baron (a fast maturing variety with round, dark green leaves).
- Elan (a large leaved variety, suitable for growing under glass and plastic).
- Verte de Cambrai (a small compact variety).
- Vit (a large leafed variety, very quick to grow, my favourite).

COURGETTE

Latin name: *Cucurbita pepo*
Family: *Cucurbitaceae*

Courgettes are an excellent crop for protected cropping. The yield is substantially higher compared to outdoor production and you can get a much earlier harvest.

Two plants are sufficient to give you a fairly large amount of courgettes for many months. Courgettes are the young immature fruits and when left to grow they turn into marrows. They usually bear dark green fruits but try some yellow and pale green varieties as well. They are delicious.

SOIL AND SITE

Courgettes need a fertile, free-draining soil which can hold plenty of moisture. A generous application of well-decomposed compost is beneficial (about 1 bucket per square metre).

They need to be positioned in full sun in the tunnel or greenhouse.

SOWING

Mid March is the earliest time you can sow courgettes. If you want to be more on the safe side you can delay until April. I sow individual seeds into 7cm pots. Ideally, the pots are left in a propagator in the greenhouse (20°C) or on a south-facing windowsill at home. The plants usually germinate within a week and start growing quickly. Four to five weeks after sowing they tend to be ready for planting into the tunnel or greenhouse. If there is a cold spell during this time you may be better off potting the plants on into 10cm pots and they can be held a couple of weeks longer on the heating bench or in the house. A late sowing in June will often produce an excellent crop from late summer until the first frost.

SPACING

Courgette plants will become very large so do not underestimate the space they require. The ideal planting distance is 1 metre. It is important to stick to this spacing but you can interplant some lettuce or annual spinach into the gaps. They can be harvested before the courgette plants fill out and require the space.

PLANT CARE

Apart from regular harvesting and keeping the weeds down there is very little else to do. If you notice that your plants look a bit stunted you can sprinkle some organic poultry pellets around the plants to provide the plants with a quick boost of energy.

It is beneficial to cut off the lower leaves of the plants as soon as they discolour. Beware though, some people develop a rash on the hands and arms when they scratch the tiny spines on the underside of the leaves. I would recommend that people sensitive to this choose a spineless variety or wear adequate protection (gloves and long sleeves). At the beginning of the cropping season, you should remove any fallen flowers and any misshaped fruits as they are likely to be the cause of grey mould.

Hand pollination

In cold, wet weather (when few insects are around) you can pollinate the flowers by hand. This will increase the chance to get fruits.

Courgette plants have separate male and female flowers. They are easily distinguished by looking at the flower stalk. The male stalk is plain and the female flower carries a small fruit on the stalk.

You transfer the pollen from the male to the female flowers with a soft brush or remove the male flower and rub it onto the open blooms of the female flowers.

Fig. 7. Hand pollination.

Note

In spring there are more male flowers produced and as day length increases more female flowers appear.

Some varieties are parthenocarpic. This simply means they can produce fruits in the absence of male flowers. No pollination is necessary and thus they are an excellent choice for early sowings under cover as there may not be enough insects around to pollinate and you may be too busy to perform this task for them.

HARVESTING

Courgettes from the early sowing will be ready in early June and they may keep cropping until October. Harvest courgettes as soon as they are the size you require. In fact, you may have to harvest them about 3 times per week. Try to cut the fruit carefully with a sharp knife at the stalk without damaging the plant. It is best not to leave overgrown courgettes (marrows) on the plants as this will sap all the energy from it and reduce the production of new fruits.

STORING

Courgettes do not store for more than a week in the fridge.

POTENTIAL PROBLEMS

There are very few problems with courgettes. The main problem occurs if there is a frosty night after you planted them into the tunnel or greenhouse. Even a light touch of frost will wipe them out. So be prepared and cover the plants with a double layer of fleece during cold spells.

At the end of the season plants may get attacked by powdery mildew. There is no cure for it but it does not kill the plant. Grey mould is a more serious disease at it can kill the plants.

HOW MUCH TO GROW?

Two plants are more than sufficient for a large family.

VARIETIES

- Ambassador F1 (high yielding dark green fruits over a long period).
- Parador F1 (an excellent yellow courgette, highly prolific and delicious).
- Cavili F1 (all female, parthonocarpic, pale green fruit).
- Defender F1 (very early, high yielding dark green fruits).
- Kojak F1 (spineless plants, high yield of dark green fruit).
- Parthenon F1 (all female, parthenocarpic, self fertile, ideal for early sowings).
- Satellite F1 (a round courgette, quite unusual).
- Tempra F1 (an early high yielding variety, compact plants).

CUCUMBER

Latin name: *Cucumis sativus*
Family: *Cucurbitaceae*

In my opinion, cucumbers are the most prolific and rewarding greenhouse or tunnel crop of all. From one single plant, provided it is well grown – you can expect to harvest well over 50 delicious cucumbers.

There is one very important thing to remember though – cucumbers are tropical plants so spoil them with warmth and moisture.

Cucumbers can grow very quickly but they can also die quickly if conditions are wrong.

SOIL AND SITE
Cucumbers love warmth, high humidity and very high soil fertility. Just imagine a plant that grows to well over 2m tall and produces

dozens of large fruits. It really needs to be well fed. I usually incorporate plenty of very well rotted compost or manure into the beds about a month before planting. Always plant them in full light with no shading from neighbouring plants.

SOWING

It is crucial that you only sow "all female" F1 hybrids. Open pollinated varieties have both male and female flowers and quite unlike most other plants, the cucumber can produce fruit from unpollinated flowers. The trouble with pollinated fruit is that they are bitter, tough skinned, full of hard seeds and with a "belly" at the end. So keep the males away from the cucumbers! If you do grow a variety that also produces male flowers you have to remove the male flowers before they open every day.

As cucumbers are heat loving and quick growing plants I delay sowing until mid April and make a second sowing in late May. I sow seeds individually into small pots (7cm) and place the pots into a propagator (21°C) or on a warm windowsill. The seeds germinate quickly within 5 days. About 2–3 weeks after sowing, the plants are ready to be potted on into a bigger (12cm) pot using a more fertile potting compost. The plants should remain in a warm place until planting.

PLANTING

When the plants are well rooted in the 12cm pots before they get pot-bound they can be planted into their final growing position in the greenhouse or polytunnel. I train the plants up strings that are attached to an overhead wire so when I plant them I first dig a big enough planting hole and then lay the bottom part of the string into the hole with the end sticking up, then take the cucumber plant out of the pot and place it over the string and gently firm it in leaving no air pockets around the roots. It is advisable not to plant cucumbers too deep or even to let the top of the compost stick out a bit. This reduces the risk of stem rot.

SPACING
Plants should be spaced 60cm apart in the row and only a single row should be planted per bed.

PLANT CARE
Just remember: cucumbers need a tropical environment so regular misting with warm water especially during the day is highly beneficial. On a weekly basis you should gently wind the main stem of the plant around the upright string and remove all side-shoots. The side-shoots grow from the joint between the leaves and the stem and so do the fruits. Ensure that you don't remove the little cucumbers.

All the fruit from the bottom 30cm should be removed while still small otherwise the cucumbers will lie on the ground and get eaten by slugs or infected by diseases. This early fruit removal enables the plants to grow stronger.

As soon as you notice that the leaves of the cucumbers lose their vigour you can sprinkle some organic poultry pellets around the base of the plants, to provide the plants with a quick boost of energy, but make sure the pellets do not touch the stems. I usually do this in July.

LAYERING
When the plants reach the top of the string and have yielded a substantial amount of fruit they can be layered. This will prolong their productive season. Unfortunately many gardeners are not aware of this and tend to give up on their crop. You simply prune all the leaves except from the top 75cm of the plants. Then you untie the string from the overhead wire and lay the plants flat on

the ground towards one side of the bed. Tie an extension to the string so it will reach the wire again. Just leave 75cm of the plant to stick up and spread a layer of a good compost/soil mixture (about 15cm deep) over the laid cucumber stems. The plants will root at each node and start growing up again and hopefully yielding a few dozen more cucumbers.

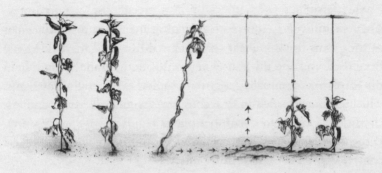

Fig. 8. Layering cucumbers.

HARVESTING

There are few things that are more impressive than the yield of cucumbers. Every day each plant produces a new cucumber during the high season. Use a sharp knife or secateurs to cut them off. Cucumbers are ready when the ends of the fruits are roundish. It is important that you harvest the crop regularly. Over mature fruit will substantially lower the overall yield and encourage plant diseases.

HOW MUCH TO GROW?

In theory one plant is more than sufficient, but I always grow at least two in case I have a casualty.

POTENTIAL PROBLEMS

Frost damage
Any touch of cold and your cucumber plants will suffer. The slightest frost will kill them and don't forget that an unheated greenhouse or polytunnel provides very little frost protection.

Red spider mite
These are serious pests especially in a greenhouse or polytunnel. They are difficult to spot with the naked eye. They form fine webs so they cross from one leaf to another. Mites feed by sucking sap from the leaves and this causes yellow spotting on the upper side of the leaves and eventually leads to complete yellowing of the leaves which become covered in fine cobwebs. As mites thrive in dry, hot conditions spray your cucumber plants regularly with warm water. If the problem recurs every year you should introduce a biological control that feeds on red spider mites.

Stem rot
Stem rot is a fairly common problem with cucumbers. Infected plants rot away at the base. To prevent this, always rotate cucumbers and never plant them in cold wet soil. As mentioned above it helps to plant them slightly raised above soil level.

VARIETIES
- Crystal Lemon (a really unique type of cucumber with a delicious small, round fruit, but not an 'all female' variety so don't grow them near your 'all females' as they would pollinate them).
- Flamingo F1 (all female, high yields of long dark green fruits, powdery mildew tolerant).
- Passandra F1 (all female, I grow this every year. It produces masses of small to medium sized cucumbers of excellent quality and is also resistant to mildew).

- Picolino F1 (all female, mini-cucumber ideal for snack boxes, length of fruit is only 12cm).
- Styx F1 (all female, straight fruit of high quality).
- Suprami F1 (all female, early variety with long dark green fruits resistant to grey mould and powdery mildew).

DILL

Latin name: *Anethum graveolens*
Family: *Umbelliferae* (also known as *Apiaceae*)

Dill is rapidly gaining popularity especially thanks to many celebrity chefs extolling its virtues. Dill is also such an easy and fast herb to grow. You can expect the first harvest about 8 weeks after sowing. It is a very short-lived annual. The fancy botanical term for this is 'ephemeral'. This means that you have to sow small amounts of it at regular intervals. The choice of variety is crucially important. Normal dill seed is quite unsuitable for leaf production. They are only good for growing dill seeds. For leaf production you have to choose a named variety that is slow to bolt. This may be the simple explanation why some gardeners are unsuccessful with dill.

SOIL AND SITE
Dill grows in any reasonably fertile soil with a pH of 6–7. Unlike many other herbs it can even be grown in semi-shade. Small

amounts of well rotted compost can be dug into the soil prior to planting.

SOWING

For continuity you can sow every 2–3 weeks from mid February until mid August. Plants that are ready in May to July should be planted outdoors. All other sowings can be planted in the tunnel or greenhouse.

The very early sowings in February and March should be done in modular trays and placed on a heating bench at 18°C. I generally sow a small pinch of seeds (about 5–7) per cell. The seedlings are not divided when planted out about 4 weeks later.

Later sowings can either be made in modular trays or sown directly into a well prepared fine seed bed.

SPACING

• Between rows: 25cm.
• Between plants: 15cm (groups of 5–7 plants).

PLANT CARE

It is important to keep dill growing steadily otherwise it is prone to bolting. This can be achieved by keeping the soil moist and the tunnel or greenhouse well ventilated.

HARVESTING

With successional sowings you can expect to harvest dill from April until mid October. You can either pick individual leaves if only small quantities are required or you can use the cut-and-come-again technique. You can expect to get two to three good cuts per plant. As soon as the new batch is producing well it is best to discard the older ones.

POTENTIAL PROBLEMS
Dill grows quite healthily throughout most of the year. Only the early and very late sowings may develop some moulds.

HOW MUCH TO GROW?
You will get 24 plants (groups of 5–7) per square metre. Each group may yield up to 30g. Sowing three cells every 2–3 weeks should be adequate for a family's needs.

VARIETIES
As mentioned above, it is crucial to choose the right variety. I have always grown the variety 'Dukat' which is very slow to run to seed. There is a new variety called 'Diane' which looks very promising too.

ENDIVE

Latin name: *Cichorium endivia*
Family: *Compositae* (also known as *Asteraceae)*

Endive is becoming increasingly popular especially the frilly leafed types as a valuable ingredient in salad bags. It is very easy to grow and is more or less free of pests and diseases. Endive grows well outside so it should only be grown indoors to extend the growing season in spring and autumn.

TYPES OF ENDIVE
There are two types of endives: broad leafed and frilly types. I personally prefer the more attractive frisee types but the broad leafed varieties tend to be hardier.

SOIL AND SITE
Endive will grow on any reasonably fertile soil. Well-decomposed compost can be incorporated.

SOWING
Endive is best sown in modular trays (1cm deep) at 18°C. I only sow 1–2 seeds per module and remove one of the doubles and prick

it out into an empty cell. You want to end up with only one seedling per module.

The transplants are usually ready to plant out about 4 weeks after sowing and will be ready for harvesting after another 4–6 weeks.

In order to prolong the growing season in spring make a few sowings in March and April and again in summer in July and August.

SPACING
- Between plants: 30cm.
- Between rows: 30cm.

PLANT CARE
Plants should be kept moist at all times as dry soil will encourage bolting. Many of the older varieties require blanching, which simply means excluding the light from plants. This reduces bitterness and makes the leaves more tender. Some of the modern varieties do not necessarily require blanching.

The recommended way for blanching is to pull the outer leaves together and tie with a string about 2 weeks before harvest and then place a plate over the whole head. I have never done it this way. I find it much easier to cover the whole plant with a bucket about 10 days before harvesting. Just cover a few plants at a time.

HARVESTING AND STORING
Cut the whole heads when mature and blanched or use individual leaves from immature plants. Once harvested, it should be consumed as soon as possible. Endive will keep in a plastic bag in the fridge for a week but only if it was harvested early in the morning.

POTENTIAL PROBLEMS
Apart from slugs, snails and aphids, endive is a very healthy crop.
   Bolting often occurs if sown too early.

HOW MUCH TO GROW?
In one square metre you get 12 plants.

VARIETIES
Curly leafed varieties (Frisee types)
- Fine Maraichere (finely cut curled leaves).
- Glory (finely serrated leaves on loose hearting heads).
- Jeti (upright leaves, easy to blanch).
- Pancalieri (self blanching type, frizzy leaves, rose tinted midrib).

Broad leafed (Scarole types)
- Avance (attractive, high yielding, cold tolerant).
- Nuance (well filled hearts, excellent quality, resistant to tipburn).

FLORENCE FENNEL
OR BULB FENNEL

Latin name: *Foeniculum vulgare* var. *azoricum*
Family: *Umbelliferae* (also known as *Apiaceae*)

Florence fennel is a Mediterranean vegetable so it will thrive in the summer heat of your tunnel or greenhouse. It is one of the most attractive vegetables with its decorative feathery foliage and the white bulb just above ground level.

I am often surprised why garden designers never use Florence fennel in their flower borders. It is also a delicious vegetable with a lovely texture and fresh taste – a hint of aniseed and celery. Apparently the Greeks and Romans ate it in order to ward off obesity.

SOIL AND SITE
Florence fennel grows well on any fertile, free-draining and moisture-retentive soil with well-decomposed compost dug into it. The ideal pH is 6.0–7.0.

It should be grown in full sun with no shading effect from neighbouring crops.

SOWING

Fennel dislikes root disturbance, so it should be sown directly into modular trays (one seed per module) about 1cm deep. The trays should be placed on a heating bench at 20°C.

In order to get a regular supply, sow only small amounts every 3 weeks from early May until late July. Ensure that you use a bolt-resistant variety for the early sowings in May.

PLANTING OUT

Plant out modules about 4–5 weeks after sowing. Do not plant them deeper than they are in the modules.

SPACING

A spacing of 35 x 35cm will give you decent sized bulbs.

PLANT CARE

Keep the beds well hoed and weeded and water the plants at least twice a week.

HARVESTING

The bulbs should be ready to harvest about 3–4 months after sowing. Cut the stalk below the bulb at ground level.

It is best to trim off all the leaves. They can be used for flavouring and stock. If the leaves remain on the harvested bulb they draw out the moisture and the bulb will become soft. It is best to harvest Florence fennel as you require it in the kitchen.

STORING

The bulbs may last for a few days if left in a plastic bag in the fridge.

POTENTIAL PROBLEMS

Slugs like the young plants and aphids feed on the leaves during warm dry weather.

If carrot root fly is a serious problem in your garden it may also affect fennel.

The most difficult problem, however, is bolting. This happens especially if there is a period of cold weather after planting and also during dry spells. To reduce the risk of bolting you could delay the first sowing until early June, water regularly and use a bolt-resistant variety for early sowings.

HOW MUCH TO GROW?

You will get 9 bulbs per square metre.

VARIETIES

- Finale (early variety and slow to bolt, suitable for tunnel production).
- Romanesco (late variety with large round bulbs).
- Rondo F1(a very early and high yielding variety, excellent for protected cropping).
- Zefa Fino (high quality, bolt-resistant, solid bulbs).

GARLIC

Latin name: *Allium sativum*
Family: *Alliaceae* (commonly known as Alliums)

Garlic is one of my favourite vegetables. It is extremely well suited to growing in a tunnel or greenhouse especially for planting in the autumn. From cloves planted in October you can expect a reliable yield of bulbs in May so they will be harvested just before your tomatoes need to be planted.

In many drier areas garlic can be successfully grown outdoors over winter but if your soil becomes waterlogged you have to grow autumn garlic indoors.

You have to make sure that you choose a suitable variety for autumn planting.

SOIL AND SITE
Garlic prefers a light, free-draining soil. It is beneficial to incorporate some well-decomposed compost prior to planting the cloves. It must be grown in full sun.

PLANTING

Garlic is grown by planting individual cloves which are split off from the bulb. On average, there are around eight to ten cloves per bulb.

In order to get decent sized bulbs, plant the cloves 20–25cm apart each way. Most gardening books recommend much closer spacing of 10–15cm. With this wider spacing the bulb size will increase. The cloves are planted upright with the tips about 2cm below the surface. Only open the bulb prior to planting otherwise the cloves will dry up.

AUTUMN PLANTING

Autumn planting is far more suitable for tunnel and greenhouse production as it can fit in well with your cropping schedules. You will always find an empty patch in October and the garlic will be ready in May just in time for planting out your tomatoes.

SPRING PLANTING

Spring planting is not advisable because the garlic would only be ready in mid June which would be too late for most maincrops such as tomatoes that need to be planted in May.

SPACING

- Between plants: 20–25cm.
- Between rows: 25cm.

PLANT CARE

Apart from keeping the beds weed-free and watered there is little else to do.

HARVESTING AND STORING

Garlic is ready to harvest when leaves turn yellow-brown. Unlike onions, harvest before the stalks fall over. This is important –

otherwise the bulb opens up and it rots during storage. Dig garlic out carefully with a fork. Remove excess dirt from the root but never cut off the foliage unless you eat it straight away.

Garlic should ideally be dried in the sun for 3–4 weeks. It can hang in the tunnel or greenhouse in the summer.

When the garlic is fully dried it can be tied into bunches. The longer the tops stay on, the longer the storage life. Air movement is essential. Store as cool and dry as possible. Relative humidity must be below 70 per cent to prevent mould. The lower the temperature, the longer the storage life. Storage at high temperatures (e.g. room temperature) is satisfactory but for shorter periods.

POTENTIAL PROBLEMS
Garlic is susceptible to the same diseases as onion but there are fewer insect problems.

PESTS
Garlic has very little pest problems. Its strong oil and natural chemicals actually repel pests. You can buy liquid garlic products for pest control.

DISEASES
Garlic suffers from the same diseases as other members of the allium family. Thus it is essential to stick to a proper rotation. There is no cure – only prevention.

HOW MUCH TO GROW?
You will get 16 bulbs per square metre.

VARIETIES
Autumn types
• Albigensian Wight (white softneck type with purple tinge).

- Early Wight (produced on the Isle of Wight, the earliest maturing garlic, purple skin).
- Solent Wight (another excellent variety from the Isle of Wight, matures late, stores very well).

GHERKIN

Latin name: *Cucumis sativus* and *Cucumis anguria*
Family: *Cucurbitaceae*

Pickled gherkins are a great addition to any sandwich.

Gherkins are very easily grown in the greenhouse or polytunnel. They are also referred to as 'cornichons' which is the French word for gherkin.

Gherkins are usually the fruit of certain cultivars of *Cucumis sativus* – the cucumber. They usually produce small fruits that should be harvested when about 5–8cm long.

There is also another type of gherkin that can be grown in a greenhouse or polytunnel. It is the West Indian Burr Gherkin (*Cucumis anguria*) which is more often grown as a plant curiosity. It has palmately lobed leaves with toothed edges and prickly fruits.

SOIL AND SITE

Gherkins prefer a sunny spot in your polytunnel or greenhouse and the soil needs to be enriched with plenty of well rotted manure or compost.

SOWING

Seeds should be sown individually into small pots (7cm) using a seed compost in late April and placed on a heating bench or a south-facing windowsill in a warm room. The seeds will germinate within a week and when they are well rooted in the pots they should be potted on into 12cm pots using a potting compost. The pots should remain on the heating bench or windowsill.

PLANTING

In late May/early June the plants can be planted out into the greenhouse soil. It is beneficial to grow them on small ridges to improve drainage. The plants should be trained up strings that are attached to an overhead wire. When you make the planting hole, place the end of the string into the planting hole and plant on top of the string. Do not plant deeper than the plant was in the pot.

SPACING

Between plants: 45cm.
Between rows: 75cm.

PLANT CARE

Gherkins need plenty of warmth and plenty of water. The side-shoots should be removed every week and the plants should be wound around the string.

HARVESTING

Gherkins should be harvested at least once a week or even twice otherwise they will quickly grow too big. The best use is to pickle them or use them as a snack.

POTENTIAL PROBLEMS

Gherkins may suffer from red spider mite, especially if the atmosphere in the greenhouse is too dry. Regular misting may prevent it. Regular application of a garlic and nettle spray may prevent various other common greenhouse pests and diseases.

VARIETIES

• Arena F1 (a high yielding variety with good quality dark green fruits).

Note: Beware that if you use a gherkin variety that produces male flowers it will cross pollinate with your expensive all female cucumbers and ruin them (see Cucumbers).

GROUNDNUT, AMERICAN

Latin name: *Apios americana*
Family: *Leguminosae*

The American Groundnut is a wonderfully exciting curiosity to grow in your polytunnel or large greenhouse. It originated in North America and was a staple food of the native people. It is also sometimes referred to as the 'Potato Bean'. Some historians believe that this is the 'potato' which Sir Walter Raleigh brought back from America.

It produces the most unusual tubers. They develop rhizomes with tuberous swellings at interval along the rhizome. It has the appearance of a necklace. The tubers are delicious raw or cooked, with a distinctive nutty flavour. It is a very trouble-free and easily grown plant.

SOIL AND SITE
American groundnut prefers a heavy wet soil with plenty of organic matter incorporated.

SOWING AND PLANTING
American groundnut can be grown from seed but it usually takes a few years before you can harvest it. It is much better to buy tubers and plant them in May about 10cm deep.

SPACING
• Between plants: 30cm.

PLANT CARE
As they are vigorous climbing plants I grow them just like runner beans, up a wigwam of tall bamboo canes that are tied together securely at the top. You may need to help them onto their supports.

The plants require regular heavy watering as they originate in wetland areas.

HARVESTING
When the plants die down you'll know that the tubers are ready. The tubers are the most unusual vegetable you will ever see. They will not store well once they are harvested. It is best to leave them in the ground over winter and use them as required. You can add half a wheelbarrow of soil on top of the tubers for additional frost protection.

POTENTIAL PROBLEMS
Generally the plants grow very healthily.

HOW MUCH TO GROW?
One wigwam will be sufficient as it is more of a curiosity crop.

VARIETIES
There are no known varieties of American Groundnut.

KOHLRABI

Latin name: *Brassica oleracea* (Gongylodes Group)
Family: *Brassicaceae* (also known as *Cruciferae*)

The common name derives from the German – Kohl meaning cabbage and rabi meaning turnip. In this type of cabbage the stem remains very short and swells just above ground level to form an edible corm.

Kohlrabi is one my favourite vegetables to grow, and in a tunnel or greenhouse you will get fantastic early crops from late winter/early spring sowings. There is no point growing them indoors later on when they will do just as well outside.

SOIL AND SITE
Kohlrabi requires an open, unshaded place. The soil should be reasonably fertile, free-draining and with a high water-holding capacity. A regular water supply is necessary.

SOWING

Kohlrabi can be sown in modular trays which usually are placed on a heating bench at 15–18°C in a greenhouse or tunnel. I sow one or two seeds per module about 1.5cm deep. The seeds usually germinate within 5–7 days and are ready for planting out about 4 weeks after sowing.

You can make the first sowing in late January and then again in late February and late March. The sowing in April can be planted outdoors in May.

SPACING

A spacing of 30 x 30cm will give you decent sized kohlrabi. If you prefer smaller vegetables you can space them 20cm apart in the row and 30cm between the rows.

PLANT CARE

Kohlrabi is an exception in the cabbage family. It is the only member that cannot be planted deeper than it was in the module and it should never be earthed up. If the soil touches the bottom of the corm it will rot.

Apart from regular weed control and watering there is nothing else to do.

HARVESTING

The corms can be harvested when they are the size of a tennis ball. It is often quite untrue that larger corms are tough. If your plants grow steady and become big they should still be fine. Tough, woody corms develop when the plants are stressed through a lack of nutrients or water. This rarely happens in a tunnel or greenhouse.

STORING

Kohlrabi is best harvested as required. It will keep for about 2 weeks if placed in a plastic bag in the fridge.

POTENTIAL PROBLEMS
Apart from the usual brassica problems, kohlrabi is sensitive to bolting especially if the temperature drops below 10°C for 2–3 days. This can be avoided by using bolt-resistant varieties.

HOW MUCH TO GROW?
You will get 15 kohlrabi from one square metre.

VARIETIES
• Azur Star (very early variety with attractive blue corm).
• Logo (white variety with good resistance to bolting).
• Luna (early variety with good resistance to bolting, green corm).
• Purple Danube (an excellent, high-yielding blue-purple variety).

LEEK

Latin name: *Allium porrum* or *ampeloprasum*
Family: *Alliaceae* (commonly known as Alliums)

Leeks really shouldn't be in a book on polytunnels as they are one of the most popular winter vegetables and are perfectly suited to any outdoor conditions. In fact for most of the year leeks perform a lot better outside than under protection. So this section is only for the die-hard leek lovers that can't do without them in May and June.

LEGEND AND LORE
The Emperor Nero is reported to have been nicknamed Porrophagus because of his inordinate appetite for leeks. He imagined that frequent eating of leeks improved his singing voice!

SOIL AND SITE

Leeks require a very fertile soil which should be enriched with plenty of farmyard manure or compost. The ideal pH range is between 6.5–7.5.

SOWING

For tunnel or greenhouse use I would only use an early variety. The seeds can be sown in modular trays in late January. I generally sow two seeds per cell.

PLANTING

Leeks can be planted approximately 6–8 weeks after sowing in modular trays. The modules can be planted when the roots hold the compost together in the cells. The cells should not be split up and the two seedlings should be planted together.

SPACING

- Between plants: 30cm if two plants are planted together.
- Between rows: 35cm.

PLANT CARE

As the plants grow, earth up the leeks with soil to blanch the stems. This simply means the covered part of the leek turns white. Be careful that you don't get soil into the heart of the leek.

HARVESTING

The first early leeks from the tunnel or greenhouse will be ready from May onwards. Trim off the roots at the base without cutting into the shank and trim the leaves so that they are the same length as the stem. Be careful not to scatter the soil into neighbouring leeks.

POTENTIAL PROBLEMS
Leeks are relatively trouble-free especially these quick growing early ones. Once ready though you have to harvest them otherwise they will bolt.

HOW MUCH TO GROW?
You will get 18 leeks per square metre.

VARIETIES
• The variety Roxton F1 is fabulous. It is very early, has dark green erect leaves.

Baby Leeks
There is a trend or fashion in all things small. Many restaurants demand baby leeks. Baby leeks can easily be produced by decreasing the spacing to about 10cm each way. That means you could get 100 baby leeks per square metre.

LEMON VERBENA

Latin name: *Aloysia citriodora, Aloysia triphylla, Lippia citriodora*
Family: *Verbenaceae*

Lemon verbena is definitely my favourite tea herb. The scent of the plant is the most refreshing, gentle delightful lemon aroma. Even just walking past the plant will make you stop in your tracks. It shouldn't be confused with lemon balm, which is a common garden herb and can easily be grown outside.

Lemon verbena originates in South America. Medicinally it is used to treat fevers and headaches and its calming and relaxing properties can help induce sleep.

I love it as a tea. You simply pick a few leaves and pour boiling water over it and you have the nicest cup of tea imaginable.

Unfortunately the plants are not hardy so they should be grown in pots and moved into a frost-free place in winter.

SOWING
Lemon verbena plants can be purchased from good garden centres. Alternatively they can be raised from seed. The seeds can be sown

any time in early spring. However seeds are not easily available. I would sow about 10 seeds into a 9cm pot using seed compost and cover with 1cm of compost. When the first true leaves appear, the seedlings should be pricked out into small pots (7cm) or large modules using potting compost. The plants can be potted on into bigger pots and then planted into the greenhouse soil.

PLANT CARE

The plants can either be grown in the greenhouse soil or in large pots. It is important that the plants do not get pot-bound so they should be potted on a few times per year. Growing the plants in pots has the advantage that they can be moved into a frost-free place in winter as the plants would not survive a winter in a tunnel or greenhouse. The ideal winter condition should be a temperature of above 3°C and below 10°C as well as a bright space such as a conservatory. If no bright frost-free place is available the plants can be put in a dark but frost-free garage. The plants will lose their leaves but will recover quickly in spring. They can be moved back into the greenhouse or polytunnel after the winter in March and should be pruned back heavily to about half the height and potted on into a larger pot.

HARVESTING

It is important to harvest lemon verbena properly. The worst thing you can do is pick individual leaves from the plant as you'll end up with a bare plant. It is much better to cut or prune shoots about 10–15cm long as this will encourage more side-shoots.

HOW MUCH TO GROW?

One plant is usually sufficient until you become addicted.

VARIETIES

There are no named varieties available.

LETTUCE

Latin name: *Lactuca sativa*
Family: *Compositae*

With the help of a greenhouse or polytunnel you can harvest lettuce for over ten months of the year. It is a wonderful and flexible crop especially suited for early spring and autumn cropping.

TYPES OF LETTUCE

Butterhead

Butterheads were the only commonly known lettuce for a long time. They form a heart with soft, delicate leaves. They have the reputation of tasting quite bland, but some varieties of butterhead, especially if organically grown, can taste quite nice. They are not suitable for the cut-and-come-again system.

Crisphead

Crispheads (or Iceberg) have become very popular in the last twenty years or more. They form a large firm, crisp and succulent heart. Again, their reputation for blandness makes them unattractive for home gardeners. However, if organically grown, and choosing the right variety, they can make an excellent salad.

Cos

The Cos lettuce forms a dark green, upright, elongated heart. The leaves are long, crisp and sweet. To my mind they are the tastiest lettuces available. Some varieties of Cos, however, are susceptible to a disorder called tipburn during the summer months. The smaller relative, Little Gem, is the most popular type.

Loose leaf

These lettuces do not form hearts thus making them suitable for picking individual leaves as required. They mature quickly and are very easy to grow. There are hundreds of varieties, which include Lollo Rossa and Bionda, Red and Green Salad Bowl.

Batavia

Batavia lettuces are a fairly new introduction. They are a cross between butterhead and crisphead lettuce. Most varieties are attractive looking and very tasty with lovely crunchy leaves.

Stem lettuce (Celtuce)

The name celtuce derives from Celery and Lettuce (CELery-letTUCE). It is grown for its edible stem which can reach up to 80cm. The heart of the stem has a delicious nutty flavour. Celtuce is a very popular vegetable in Asia, but is still virtually unknown in Europe. Seeds are available from a few seed companies and it can be grown quite easily here.

Note: Many people believe that rocket, mizuna, mustards or cresses belong to the lettuce family. This is not the case. It is important to remember that they are in the brassica family and should be grown in the brassica section of the rotation.

SOIL AND SITE

The soil should be reasonably fertile. A pH of 6.5–7.5 is ideal. Only well-decomposed compost should be used.

SOWING

I generally sow lettuce seeds in modular trays. If I want a head of lettuce, only one seed per cell is required. For cut-and-come-again lettuce I generally sow 3–5 seeds per cell. Lettuce needs light to germinate, so do not cover the seeds with compost. In your polytunnel or greenhouse you can start sowing lettuce in late January and continue on with successional sowings until August. During late spring and summer, lettuce will grow better outdoors.

There are also varieties available that can overwinter indoors and are ready in early spring. Because of the disease problem of overwintering lettuce, I prefer to grow the more hardier orientals during the winter months.

During hot spells move the trays into a cool shed for 2 days and then back into the tunnel. At 18°C lettuce will germinate after 3–4 days.

Remember that lettuce seeds won't germinate if the temperature of the compost is above 25°C. The seeds develop a dormancy and germination occurs only weeks later and then is very patchy.

TIMING

From sowing to planting out: 3–5 weeks depending on the season and the weather.

From planting to harvesting: 4–6 weeks.

PLANTING

The seedlings should be planted with their seed leaves (cotyledons) just above ground level. If your seedlings do get a bit leggy you can safely plant them a little bit deeper in order to cover the stem but only up to the seed leaves. The plants definitely seem to appreciate this extra care. But never plant the seedlings below the cotyledons. If the growing point of the plant is buried it will rot away.

SPACING

Small lettuce (Little Gem)
- Between plants: 20cm.
- Between rows: 20cm.

Medium lettuce (Lollo types, butterheads etc)
- Between plants: 25cm.
- Between rows: 25cm.

Large lettuce (Iceberg)
- Between plants: 35cm.
- Between rows: 35cm.

ROTATION

Lettuce is an ideal plant for filling in gaps. It can be planted between widely spaced crops such as courgettes and can be harvested before the courgette needs that space. If you have any spare space anywhere in your tunnel or greenhouse you can happily plant lettuce there. On the other hand you should avoid planting lettuce in the same place every year to prevent a build up of pests and diseases, especially the lettuce root aphid.

PLANT CARE

It is important to keep your lettuces weed-free at all times and avoid spilling earth onto the leaves while weeding.

HARVESTING AND STORING

There are three ways of harvesting lettuce:

1. Cut the whole plant when fully mature.
2. Pick individual leaves from the outside of the plant as required (only for leafy lettuce).
3. Cut a loose-leafed lettuce about 5cm above the growth point and it will grow new leaves that can be cut again within the next 3 weeks. The plant should be cut before it has fully matured.

Tip

Harvest lettuce at sunrise! The earlier in the day you harvest your lettuce the longer it keeps and the more nutritious it is. If you harvest lettuce at 6am and put it in a plastic bag in the fridge it will keep for a week as fresh as when harvested. If you harvest lettuce on a sunny day at 2pm it has already wilted as water has evaporated from the leaves and the sunnier the day the more water evaporates.

POTENTIAL PROBLEMS

Pests

Leatherjackets

Leatherjackets are the larvae of the cranefly (daddy longlegs). These are the louts of your vegetable patch as they just eat through the stem of newly planted lettuce moving along the row leaving a trail of destruction. It is important to check your newly planted seedlings regularly and inspect the soil under each destroyed lettuce, picking up the larvae before they move onto the next plant. You can then replant the empty space with a spare lettuce.

They are abundant in grassland so anybody with a new garden is sure to encounter them.

Cutworms

Cutworms are the larvae of some moth species. They do similar damage as the leatherjackets but are less common.

Slugs and snails
You can spread Ferramol organic slug pellets around newly planted crops.

Leaf aphids
Every year you will get a spell when aphids suck out the juice of your lettuce. Most of the time, the damage is not severe and you can simply rinse them off. Leaf aphids can be prevented by a weekly spray of garlic water. It only works if you spray before aphids appear. There are also aphid-resistant varieties available.

Root aphids
Root aphids are likely to be more of a problem in the tunnel or greenhouse because generally less attention is paid to crop rotation.

You notice them when you pull up a sick looking lettuce plant and you find white powdery dust with small white aphids all around the roots. Once you have it, there is no cure for this lettuce. To prevent further outbreaks, try the following combination of methods:

• Rotate your lettuce.
• Use a tolerant variety.
• Remove lettuce plants and roots when ready. Do not leave bolted or old lettuce in the ground.

Diseases
The two most common diseases in lettuce are downy mildew (Bremia) and grey mould (Botrytis). There are now many mildew-resistant varieties available and grey mould can be avoided if the lettuces are grown in a clean weed-free environment and adequate ventilation is provided. As a prevention avoid watering late in the evening as this encourages fungal diseases.

Disorders
Tip burn
Tip burn is a physiological disorder associated with a lack of calcium, especially if the soil is too dry. The plants lose more water

than they can absorb, causing a browning of the leaf edges. The plants will eventually rot.

Generally lettuce plants suffer more in a greenhouse or polytunnel. There is no cure for it, but luckily there are now many varieties that are less susceptible to tipburn. As a prevention mist the atmosphere in the greenhouse or polytunnel in late morning on hot days. You can do this by simply spraying the water around the air.

Leggy seedlings

Lettuce seedlings are prone to become leggy. The reason is generally lack of light. So make sure that your propagation area is in full sun. Leggy seedlings are weaker and the plants are thus more prone to pests and diseases.

HOW MUCH TO GROW?

Most people sow too many seeds in one go and have a massive glut at some point with nothing afterwards. From one sowing they will all ripen around the same time and will only last for a week or two before they bolt.

A little planning will provide you with lettuce for many months. For example if you eat 5 heads of lettuce per week sow 15 seeds every fortnight. The 5 extras are spares for potential slug or leatherjacket casualties.

VARIETIES
Butterhead
- Buttercrunch (a cross between a butterhead and a crisphead, with a crunchy heart and soft outer leaves).
- Marvel of four seasons (very attractive red-green variety, very popular).
- Matilda (fast growing and aphid-resistant variety).
- Roxy (an attractive, shiny red butterhead, slow to bolt, resistant to tipburn).

• Sylvesta (reliable butterhead, resistant to tipburn, leaf aphids and downy mildew).

Loose Leaf
• Crosby (a much improved Lollo Bionda type with excellent disease resistance).
• Aruba (a red salad bowl type with an excellent colour and compact habit).
• Bergamo (a Lollo Bionda type, slow to bolt, very early).
• Catalogna Cerbiatta (a highly ornamental oak leaf variety with deeply lobed leaves).
• Eraclea (early, green oak leaf type).
• Fristina (very curly leaves and an excellent crisp texture).
• Matador (a triple red Lollo Rossa variety, resistant to downy mildew).
• Verdes (green oak leaf, slow to bolt, resistant to tipburn, leaf aphids and downy mildew).

Crisphead (or Iceberg)
• Ardinas (dark colour, slow bolting and strong against tipburn).
• Argentinas (well shaped iceberg, good all round disease resistance).
• Brandon (high quality variety with excellent mildew resistance, produces large dense heads).
• Dublin (a reliable variety with round solid heads).
• Iceberg (very large crisp white hearts).
• Lakeland (forms tight heads even in poor summers).
• Saladin (an excellent and reliable variety).

Cos
• Chatsworth (one of the sweetest tasting lettuce, with bubbly textured pale green leaves).

- Little Gem Delight (an improved Little Gem type produces compact heads with a sweet nutty taste).
- Pinokkio (dark green medium sized cos lettuce with crisp hearts).
- Rafael (a mini cos, strong against bolting and tipburn).
- Red Cos (one of my favourite cos types with deep burgundy red, waxy thick leaves).
- Rusty (unusual large dark red cos).
- Seville (very attractive red cos).

Batavia
- Campania (light green colour and open, but well filled hearts; tolerant to tip burn).
- Red and Green Batavia (excellent mixture of red and green batavia lettuce, quick to mature, mildew-resistant).
- Roger (fast growing reddish brown batavia lettuce with crunchy leaves).

MELON

Latin name: *Cucumis melo*
Family: *Cucurbitaceae*

Melons are such an exciting crop for a polytunnel or greenhouse if you live in the warmer parts of the country. Growing and harvesting melons will be the highlight of your gardening year.

Unfortunately in more northern parts you will need an exceptionally nice summer so the harvest will be quite unpredictable.

SOIL AND SITE
Melons are true sun lovers. There can't be any shading from any neighbouring crop. They also require a fertile soil so plenty of well-decomposed compost or manure should be incorporated prior to planting. The soil should be free-draining as well as moisture retentive.

SOWING

Seeds should be sown individually into small pots (7cm) using a seed compost in mid April. Place the pots on a heating bench (23°C) or a south-facing windowsill in a warm room. The seeds usually germinate within a week and when they are well rooted in the pots (about 3 weeks later) they should be potted on into 12cm pots using a potting compost. The pots should remain on the heating bench or windowsill until they are ready to plant out into the greenhouse around early June. Commercially melons are grafted onto more vigorous as well as disease-resistant rootstocks.

PLANTING

In late May or early June the plants can be planted out into the greenhouse soil. It is beneficial to grow them on small ridges to improve drainage.

SPACING

- Between plants: 45cm.
- Between rows: 90cm.

PLANT CARE

Melons need plenty of warmth and plenty of water. They can either be trained upright on strings, trellis or some strong netting or alternatively they can trail along on the ground. I prefer to have them train upwards otherwise they are very prone to slug damage and also weed control is inhibited.

The fruits are usually produced on the side-shoots. You shouldn't leave more than one fruit per side-shoot or six to ten in total per plant.

The main growing shoot should be cut off after the fifth leaf. This encourages primary side-shoots. The primary side-shoots should be pruned after they have produced four leaves. Finally on these secondary side-shoots the melons are formed. Only leave one fruit per side-shoot and prune the shoots about five leaves after each fruit. The fruits of certain varieties can become very heavy and may pull the whole plant down. It is very important to support the fruit with a sling or by tying the side-shoots to the supports.

You shouldn't leave too many fruits on each plant. The number of fruits that will ripen depends on the climate, the summer and the variety. You may only get 4–6 fruits per plant. If you are lucky you may get 10 melons.

HARVESTING
Melons will be ready from late summer onwards. To check if they are ready, gently press the skin at the end of the fruit and, if it gives a little, the melon is ready to harvest. Cut the fruit with the handle still attached. You could leave the melon in the house for a few days to complete ripening.

POTENTIAL PROBLEMS
Melons may suffer from fungal diseases such as mildew and grey mould. As a prevention avoid watering the plants in late evening as this encourages the spread of fungal diseases. If the plants are already affected you can spray with a milk/water solution.

VARIETIES
- Blenheim Orange (old variety, orange flesh and good flavour).
- Emir F1 (round to oval shaped and slightly ribbed fruit, tolerant to low temperatures, very tasty and sweet, resistant to downy mildew).
- Ogen (green fleshed reliable Canteloupe type).
- Sweetheart F1 (an excellent, reliable variety with white fruits, Canteloupe type).

OCA

Latin name: *Oxalis tuberosa*
Family: *Oxalidaceae*

Oca is a wonderful vegetable for the polytunnel and greenhouse. In some years indoor crops are the only reliable ones as oca is daylength sensitive. It only forms tubers late in the autumn when the day length is less than 9 hours, so a polytunnel or greenhouse is advantageous as it prolongs the growing season.

Oca resembles the native wood sorrel (also an *Oxalis*) and develops lovely yellow flowers in late summer. Oca is the second most widely grown root crop for millions of traditional highlanders in the Andes. It has been cultivated there since ancient times. The Incas have developed many diverse varieties. It is such an easy crop to grow and is virtually free from any pests and diseases.

SOIL AND SITE

Oca requires only a reasonably fertile soil with a slightly acid to neutral pH. It will grow in full sun but can also cope with some shade from taller growing crops such as tomatoes or cucumbers.

SOWING

Oca tubers can be planted directly into the tunnel or greenhouse as soon as they start to sprout in storage. This usually occurs around early April.

SPACING

Between plants: 30cm.
Between rows: 40cm.

PLANT CARE

It is beneficial to earth up the stalks just as with potatoes. Regular watering is essential.

HARVESTING AND STORING

Ocas should not be harvested until the frost has killed off the leaves as they do most of their tuber development at the end of the season. Ocas may be stored for several months in boxes of sand in a cool frost-free shed.

POTENTIAL PROBLEMS

There are really no pests or diseases which trouble ocas.

HOW MUCH TO GROW?

As the tubers are difficult and very expensive to obtain I would start growing just a few to see if you like them. Each planted tuber will yield up to 15 tubers in the autumn. You should save the best ones for replanting the following year.

VARIETIES

Although in the Andes there are many different types of oca, they don't have English variety names. They come in different shapes and sizes. The colours range from yellow, red, purple to almost black. We only have the yellow and red type here.

ONION

Latin name: *Allium cepa*
Family: *Alliaceae* (commonly known as alliums)

Growing onions under cover may seem strange to many gardeners as they do well outdoors. The only time it makes sense to grow them in a tunnel or greenhouse is from an autumn planting and a harvest in May. Only plant as many as you need to bridge the gap until your spring planted onions are ready in July or August. So this section will only cover the autumn planted Japanese onions.

SOIL AND SITE

Onions require a reasonably fertile soil with a good tilth. They should not be fed with fresh or semi-decomposed manure. A dressing of well-decomposed garden compost is beneficial. The ideal pH for onions is 6.5–7.5 so you may have to apply ground limestone or, even better, calcified seaweed if your soil is acidic. Onions prefer a sunny site.

SOWING AND PLANTING

Growing from sets

Japanese onion sets can be planted from September to October. Sets are small immature onions. You simply plant the small bulbs so that the top half of the bulb is still showing above ground. Only plant good quality onion sets. They should be firm, rounded, no shoots or roots visible and of small to medium size.

Growing from seed

Many gardeners believe that onions grown from seed are healthier and less likely to bolt. I found this to be true in some years but not in others. If growing from seed the choice of varieties is a lot better than from sets.

Overwintering Japanese onions should be sown in the second week of August. I usually sow 4 seeds per cell in a modular tray and place the tray on a heating bench in a greenhouse or polytunnel. They are ready for planting into the tunnel or greenhouse around 6–8 weeks later. Each module is planted undisturbed – the seedlings are not separated.

SPACING

Seeds

Modular grown seedlings (4 seeds per module) are spaced 30 x 30cm apart each way.

Sets

Onion sets are spaced 25cm between rows and 10cm in the row. If you want to impress your neighbours simply plant them 15cm apart in the row and you will get enormous onions but the yield per square metre will drop significantly.

You can also plant four sets close together in a block and space each block 30cm apart each way like the modular grown seedlings.

PLANT CARE

Apart from regular hoeing and weeding there is little else to do. Be careful, however, that you do not hoe too deeply as onions have a very shallow root system. You may be better off hand weeding at the later stages.

HARVESTING

The overwintered onions from the tunnel or greenhouse should be harvested and dried in May. You should aim to use them up before the spring planted crop is ready in late July as overwintering onions do not store well.

POTENTIAL PROBLEMS

There are not as many problems associated with growing onions over winter. Birds are less likely to be a nuisance in the tunnel or greenhouse and there are also fewer diseases. However in order to avoid the most serious onion disease – white rot – you should be strict about your crop rotation with regards to the onion family. This also includes scallions, leeks and garlic.

HOW MUCH TO GROW?

You will get 40 onions per square metre.

VARIETIES

- Despina F1 (high yielding early variety, produces round bulbs, downy mildew-resistant).
- Senshyu (an open-pollinated variety, slightly elongated globe shape).
- Toughball F1 (globe shaped, medium early, good resistance to grey mould and downy mildew).

ORIENTAL MUSTARD

Latin name: *Brassica juncea*
Family: *Brassicaceae*

Oriental mustards are starting to become very popular. They make an excellent addition to any salads and provide beautiful colour, shape and spice. There is an ever increasing range of varieties available and their real advantage is that they are very hardy. They may be the only crop that will survive a harsh winter. In fact they are at their best if grown during the autumn, winter and spring months in a polytunnel or greenhouse.

TYPES OF ORIENTAL MUSTARDS
Frilly-leaved mustards
These are my favourites. The leaves are the most attractive leaves in a salad bowl. They are very finely serrated – more than you can imagine. There are three excellent varieties: 'Red Frills', 'Green Frills' and 'Golden Streaks'. I highly recommend any of them.

Purple large-leaved mustards

The purple mustards grow extremely fast. Before you notice it the leaves have outgrown salad size. They have a reasonably mild taste compared to the other types.

Spicy, hardy mustards

There are two excellent varieties: 'Green Wave' and 'Green-in-the-snow'. They are definitely the hardiest plants and produce an abundance of fiercely 'mustardy' leaves throughout the winter. Fantastic if you love mustard. You really get a kick when you eat the leaves.

Mizuna and mibuna

These two excellent winter salads should actually be in a class of their own. They are *Brassica rapa* var. *nipposinica*. They are both very attractive and delicious salads that can be grown successfully throughout the winter. Mizuna has glossy, serrated leaves and mibuna has very plain narrow leaves.

SOIL AND SITE

Oriental mustards do well in any reasonably fertile soil.

SOWING

The best time to sow oriental mustards for planting into the tunnel or greenhouse is in late August until early October. I usually sow 5–7 seeds in each module. The modular transplants are ready for planting out about 5 weeks after sowing.

You can make more successional sowings from late January until April but they never perform as well as the autumn sowing. They are likely to bolt prematurely and also get attacked by the fleabeetle.

SPACING
- Between rows: 25cm.
- Between plants: 20cm (5 plants per station).

PLANT CARE
It is essential to keep the plot completely weed-free and watered regularly.

HARVESTING
You can either harvest individual leaves as required or use the cut-and-come-again method: cut the whole plant at about 5cm height from the soil level and the leaves will re-grow. This procedure can be repeated within the next 2–3 weeks.

POTENTIAL PROBLEMS
Oriental mustards may suffer from all brassica diseases but the fleabeetles cause the most havoc. The symptoms are hundreds of tiny little 'shotholes' through the leaves that are caused by a tiny shiny black beetle that jumps off the leaves when disturbed. Only the autumn and late winter sowing will escape the fleabeetle. If you are determined to grow oriental mustards in spring and summer you will have to cover the beds as soon as they are planted with a fine netting such as fleece or a fine Enviromesh.

PAK CHOI

Latin name: *Brassica rapa* var. *chinensis*
Family: *Brassicaceae* (also known as *Cruciferae*)

Pak choi has become a very popular vegetable thanks to its promotion by many celebrity chefs. It is a delicious vegetable and very easy and quick to grow. It can be eaten at any stage of its development, raw or stir-fried.

Pak choi is an excellent vegetable for growing in tunnels and greenhouses especially in the latter part of the year. It is also very hardy and can be overwintered for an early spring harvest.

SOIL AND SITE
Pak choi requires a fertile and well-drained soil with good water retention and a pH range of 5.8–7. A generous application of well decomposed compost or manure is essential.

SOWING

Pak choi is an excellent follow-on crop in summer. In spring the leaves are usually destroyed by the fleabeetle. The best time to sow pak choi is from late June until mid September. I usually sow one seed per cell into a modular tray. This produces a nice single head of pak choi. If you grow them for baby leaves you can sow 4 seeds per cell. The plants are ready to transplant 3–4 weeks after sowing.

SPACING

- Between plants: 20cm.
- Between rows: 25cm.

PLANT CARE

Pak choi requires unchecked, rapid growth otherwise the plants may bolt. You need to keep the plants well watered at all times.

HARVESTING

The plants are ready to harvest about 4–8 weeks after planting, depending on the season. Plants can be harvested whole or individual leaves can be cut with a knife or scissors. The small leaves are delicious in salads and the bigger ones can be used in stir fries. The mid September sowing is definitely the best as you'll be able to harvest leaves from late October until the following March. The plants are very hardy.

POTENTIAL PROBLEMS

Pak choi may suffer from the usual brassica pests and diseases.

Fleabeetles are a particular problem especially in spring and summer. If you insist on growing pak choi early in the year you will have to cover the plants with fleece straight after planting to prevent a fleabeetle attack.

HOW MUCH TO GROW?

You will get 20 plants per square metre (single or multi-sown).

VARIETIES

My favourite varieties are:

- Joi Choi F1 (delicious high yielding variety with green leaves and pure white stems).
- Tatsoi (a small dark green type ideal for harvesting individual leaves).

PARSLEY

Latin name: *Petroselinum hortense*
Family: *Umbelliferae* (also known as *Apiaceae*)

The season for parsley can be extended by at least three months if grown under protection. In mild winters you could even harvest parsley right through the winter.

There are two types of parsley – flat leafed and curly parsley. Both types are very popular herbs.

SOIL AND SITE
Parsley prefers a rich, loamy soil with plenty of well-rotted compost added to it. The pH should be between 6.5 and 7.0.

SOWING
I usually start sowing parsley in early February. I sow 3–4 seeds into each module and place the tray on a heating bench (20°C) or alternatively in a warm sunny room in the house. The second sowing in April or May can be planted outdoors and the third

sowing is usually done in July. The last sowing will over-winter in the greenhouse or polytunnel.

SPACING
- Between plants: 20cm.
- Between rows: 25cm.

Note: Do not split up the modules. Plant the three or four seedlings together.

PLANT CARE
Keep the plants moist at all times as infrequent watering may cause the plants to bolt prematurely. Control weeds regularly as this will facilitate regular harvesting.

HARVESTING
There are two ways of harvesting parsley. You can either pick individual leaves from the outside of the plants and you can do this best by twisting the stems with a downward/side pull off the plants. It is important not to leave long pieces of stem attached to the plants as they make further harvests increasingly difficult.

The second way is the cut-and-come-again method. You simply cut the whole plant about 5cm above ground. This is a very quick method but the yield will be reduced as you inevitably harvest many small leaves from the centre. After cutting, it will take about 3 weeks before you can harvest again.

POTENTIAL PROBLEMS
Parsley is a relatively easy plant to grow. In some years the carrot root fly may cause some damage.

HOW MUCH TO GROW?
You will get 20 plants per square metre. Around 6 plants for each

of the three sowings will be more than adequate even for keen parsley lovers.

VARIETIES
- Italian Giant (a vigorous flat leaved variety with brilliant green leaves and serrated edges).
- Moss Curled (an excellent and reliable variety with very curly leaves).
- Bravour (an excellent curly variety, high yielding).

PEA

Latin name: *Pisum sativum*
Family: *Leguminosae*

Peas are not really a likely crop for a polytunnel or greenhouse. In fact, during the summer and early autumn months peas will do a lot better outside. The only time I would grow peas indoors is in late winter. I usually sow the seeds in late January and expect a first harvest in early April.

TYPES OF PEAS

There are three types of pea: the normal garden pea, mange-tout type and sugar snap. Ideally choose an early variety of your preferred type.

SOIL AND SITE

Peas grow in any reasonably fertile soil. However, they dislike an application of fresh manure. They are excellent nitrogen fixers and get lazy if too much nitrogen is applied previously. They also need a sunny spot in your greenhouse.

SOWING

Peas can be sown in small pots or in guttering pipes and placed on a heating bench. This will speed up germination during the cold period. The soil can be warmed up by covering it with black plastic for a couple of weeks prior to planting. The pots or guttering pipe can be planted into the tunnel or greenhouse border about 5 weeks after sowing. If the greenhouse soil is warm enough, the seeds can be sown directly into the border.

You can grow them in a single drill in the middle of the bed and support them with a fence or in a double row 70cm apart and erect a bamboo/branches framework. One sowing in late January/February will usually be sufficient.

I have never attempted to do a late sowing indoors to extend the growing season towards the end of the year. A July sowing is probably best for that. I would select a variety that has some resistance to mildew as peas are very prone to this disease towards the end of the year and the sheltered conditions of a tunnel or greenhouse exacerbate the problem.

SPACING
- Between plants: 5cm.
- Between rows: 70cm (if you have a double row).

PLANT CARE

Dwarf peas need little climbing support. If they are grown in closely spaced double rows they may hold each other up together.

Any stragglers can be helped with a short branch. Dwarf peas mature far earlier than taller varieties but won't last as long. This enables a gardener to get a quick crop out of an unused space before the main crops such as tomatoes or cucumbers are planted in mid May.

The tall pea varieties need to be trained up adequately. This can be done with sticks, chicken or sheep fence or bamboo canes. Peas, however, find it difficult to climb up bamboo canes, so you should use twigs in between the canes. Remember to check the height of the variety you grow and erect a high enough frame for the peas.

HARVESTING

Early peas from a tunnel can be harvested from early April until mid May when they should be cleared to allow the planting of the main crops. The pods should be picked regularly (once or twice a week), so they are still tender. If you do not harvest regularly the plants will soon stop flowering. The sowing in July will yield peas from September onwards when your outdoor crops are starting to get tired.

POTENTIAL PROBLEMS

Especially for the very early sowings mice can be a big problem. As soon as they discover the delicious seeds there is no stopping them. If you are worried about it you should raise the seeds in a safe area for planting out at a later stage.

The main disease is powdery mildew. The leaves and pods develop a sticky grey-white substance. Peas will usually develop this disease in late summer but if you grow the variety Greenshaft you will have much less of a problem.

HOW MUCH TO GROW?

You will get about 1kg of peas per square metre.

VARIETIES
Garden Peas
- Hurst Greenshaft (the one and only!).

Mangetout
- Carouby de Maussane (very tall, purple flowers).
- Delikata (very productive, resistance to mildew, 60–75cm tall).
- Garnet (a very productive early variety producing a high yield of delicious mangetout peas).
- Oregon Sugar Pod (tall growing mangetout pea with excellent flavour).
- Sweet Horizon (high quality, late maturing mangetout type, very high yields of straight, dark green pods. Mildew-resistant).
- Sugar Dwarf Sweet Green (dwarf pea, 60cm tall, suitable for early sowings).

Sugar Snap
- Sugar Ann (produces high yields of stringless sugar snaps, height 75cm).
- Sugar Snap (very sweet, round podded, up to 1.8m tall).
- Zucolla (excellent dwarf sugar snap pea with high yields, good mildew resistance, 75cm).
- Delikett (a dwarf sugar snap with compact plant habit, excellent taste, can be cropped over a long period of time, stringless peas).

Speciality Pea
- Ezeta's Kromber Blauschokker (very unusual tall growing pea with distinctive purple pods).

PEPINO

Latin name: *Solanum muricatum*
Family: *Solanaceae*

Like so many of my favourite greenhouse vegetables, pepino originates in the Andes where it is widely grown. Pepino is also known as the 'Melon Pear'. It produces a delicious sweet fruit with a slight resemblance to melons and a hint of pear. The fruit is usually eaten raw and should be peeled. I have only grown it once and had to wait a long time for the first fruits to ripen but it was well worth the long wait.

SOIL AND SITE
Pepino likes full sun but in the warmer parts of the country it can also cope with semi-shade. A fertile soil with well-decomposed compost added to it is essential.

SOWING

Pepino seeds should be sown in mid March. I usually broadcast a few seeds into a 9cm pot containing a good seed compost and only cover the seeds very lightly. The pots are placed on a heating bench (20°C) or south-facing windowsill. When the first true leaves appear, the seedlings should be pricked out into individual small (9cm) pots using a potting compost. The pots should remain on the heating bench. The plants can be planted out into the polytunnel or greenhouse in May when the danger of frost has passed.

Pepino can also easily be propagated from existing plants by taking cuttings in autumn (about 10cm long). This may be useful if you have a friend with a good plant. There is definitely some variation amongst pepino plants.

SPACING
• Between plants: 50cm.
• Between rows: 50cm.

PLANT CARE

Apart from regular watering there is very little else to do. Pepinos tend to have a sprawling habit so you may support the branches with a few twigs or plant supports.

HARVESTING

Harvest the delicious fruits when they start to turn yellow with pronounced purple stripes and when they are slightly soft to the touch.

POTENTIAL PROBLEMS

As they are closely related to the tomato and potato they suffer from the same pests and diseases. The control methods are the same as for tomatoes.

HOW MUCH TO GROW?

One or two plants are sufficient as they are more a curiosity than a crop that fills you up.

VARIETIES

Up to quite recently there were no named varieties of pepino available but this may change rapidly.

PEPPER

Latin name: *Capsicum annuum*
Family: *Solanaceae*

Peppers are a useful crop for the polytunnel or greenhouse. But don't necessarily expect to grow the large yellow or red supermarket ones. All peppers start off green and eventually turn yellow, orange, red or even purple or black as they mature. In our climate you will get a much higher yield if you harvest the peppers when they are still green. Peppers require the same growing conditions as tomatoes but the yield is much lower. One advantage, however, is that the plants won't grow more than 1m in height so they can grow at the south-facing edge bed.

SOIL AND SITE
Peppers require a very fertile and free-draining soil with a reasonable amount of well-rotted manure added to it prior to

planting. The pH should be between 6 and 7. They should be grown in full sun.

SOWING

Peppers are very slow starters so I usually sow the seeds as early as February and place the trays on a warm heating bench (20°C). The seeds are sown in a small pot or standard seed tray about 2cm apart from each other and covered with 1cm of sieved seed compost. The seedlings will appear about 2 weeks after sowing. When the first true leaf appears, the seedlings should be pricked out individually into small pots using a richer potting compost (7cm). And when they are well rooted they can be potted on into 10cm pots. They should remain on the heating bench until they are planted out into the greenhouse soil in May.

SPACING

Peppers should be spaced 45cm apart each way.

PLANT CARE

Support each plant with a bamboo cane. Water regularly and feed with comfrey liquid when fruits begin to form.

HARVESTING

Harvest peppers as soon as they are a reasonable size. The fruits should be cut using sharp secateurs. You may get between 5–15 fruits per plant, depending on the season, soil fertility and especially on the choice of variety.

POTENTIAL PROBLEMS

Peppers are susceptible to greenfly, whitefly and red spider mite. As a prevention you can spray with a garlic and nettle spray once a week.

VARIETIES

- Bell Boy F1 (a high yielding variety suitable for cold greenhouse production, good disease resistance).
- Bendigo F1 (an excellent and very reliable variety with blocky green fruits that turn red).
- Big Bertha (a large pepper, ideal for stuffing).
- Roberta F1 (an early maturing bell fruit pepper with a compact and robust plant habit).
- Sweet Chocolate (an unusual chocolate brown skinned variety).

POTATO

Latin name: *Solanum tuberosum*
Family: *Solanaceae* (Nightshade Family)

The first early potatoes in the year are one of the most anticipated crops for most gardeners. With the help of a tunnel or greenhouse you can get an early harvest of delicious potatoes as early as late April. This is just the time when your stored potatoes go soft and the price of potatoes in the shops increases.

Another advantage with such an early crop is that it is guaranteed blight-free. The potatoes will be in and out before the blight spores are flying about.

SOIL AND SITE
The soil should be fertile and free-draining. Potatoes require a generous application of well-decomposed compost or manure.

However, if too much fresh manure is incorporated the potatoes often 'grow into leaf' at the expense of producing good tubers. This problem is usually worse in a tunnel or greenhouse.

CHITTING

Buy your early seed potatoes in December and place them in shallow trays in a warm and bright room. By late January the tubers will have developed small green shoots. If you were to leave the tubers in a dark place, the shoots would become long and white and break when you tried to plant them, and so be quite useless.

It is important to harden off the tubers before planting them into the tunnel or greenhouse. You can do this by moving them out into the greenhouse during the day and back in at night for a few days. After that you can leave them in the greenhouse for another few days provided there is no frost forecast and cover them with fleece at night. Then they will be ready to plant.

PLANTING

Chitted potato tubers can be planted into the tunnel or greenhouse beds in late January until March provided it's a 'first early' variety. The tubers should be planted 10–15cm deep into fertile and well prepared ground.

SPACING
- Between plants: 25cm.
- Between rows: 50cm.

ROTATION

Potatoes are susceptible to a wide range of diseases. It's therefore essential that they follow a strict rotation programme.

Very early potatoes usually get away with relatively few problems compared to the later outdoor crops.

PLANT CARE

If there is a danger of frost and your potato shoots are just appearing you can protect them by earthing them up and covering the shoots with soil for protection.

When the haulm (shoot) is about 20cm high you should earth them up again. Use a draw hoe and pull loose soil against the haulm. Cover roughly half of the stem (10cm). Alternatively you can cover the shoots with one or two layers of fleece.

HARVESTING AND STORING

Early potatoes can be harvested whenever you feel they are big enough. From a late January planting you should get some baby potatoes in late April but the longer you can wait, the higher the yield will be. This crop will supply you with the most delicious potatoes in May and June until your early outdoor crop is ready in July.

It is important that you harvest all potatoes, even the very smallest, otherwise they will become weeds for the following crop.

POTENTIAL PROBLEMS

If you look in gardening books the list of potential potato troubles appears endless. The most common ones for early indoor production are:

Frost damage

Frost protection can be achieved by earthing up or covering the plants with fleece.

Blackleg

The symptoms include blackening of the stem at ground level and the leaves turning yellow and wilting. The disease is worse on heavy ground and during wet weather. There is no treatment for it. You should remove the diseased plants and burn them.

Common scab

The symptoms are scaly patches on the potatoes. They are, however, only on the skin, so the eating quality is not affected.

HOW MUCH TO GROW?

One square metre may yield around 5kg of potatoes.

VARIETIES

First earlies

- Sharpe's Express
- Homeguard
- Red Duke of York

Second earlies

- Catriona
- Charlotte
- Nadine
- Orla

RADISH

Latin name: *Raphanus sativus*
Family: *Brassicaceae* (also known as *Cruciferae*)

Radishes are an excellent and very fast growing, crunchy small root vegetable. They are perfect for a quick snack. Try cutting them in half and eat with a pinch of salt and butter. They are really quite delicious. Radishes grown with protection are even more tender and delicious.

SOIL AND SITE
Radishes will grow in almost any reasonably fertile soil as long as there is plenty of moisture in the soil. They do require a place in full sun. The ideal pH ranges from 6–6.5.

SOWING
Radishes are one of the fastest vegetables to mature. You can harvest the roots from about 4 to 6 weeks after sowing. The only drawback

is that once they are ready they will either become woody or go to seed. So you should only sow small quantities every now and then. Radishes are fairly hardy vegetables, so they can be sown in the tunnel or greenhouse from early February until early April every 2 weeks. The sowings from mid April until July can be made outdoors. Later sowings from late July until September can be made indoors again.

Seeds can be sown directly into the ground. They should be sown very thinly (about 2.5cm apart) in rows 15cm apart and about 1.5cm deep. Radish seeds are quite big so they can be spaced out accurately. As soon as they have all germinated you can start thinning them. For successional cropping you should sow small quantities every fortnight.

SPACING
- Row distance: 15cm.
- Distance in the row: 2–4cm.

ROTATION
It is important to keep radishes in the brassica section of your rotation to prevent a build up of the numerous brassica pests and diseases. Don't be tempted to intercrop them with other vegetables.

PLANT CARE
There is no maintenance required, apart from thinning and keeping the plot weed-free.

HARVESTING
Radishes are ready 4–6 weeks after sowing. They have to be harvested straight away otherwise they will become woody and very hot flavoured.

POTENTIAL PROBLEMS

The main pest of radishes is the fleabeetle. The symptoms are small 'shot-holes' through the leaves. A heavy infestation can destroy the crop. Covering the bed with Bionet or fleece straight after sowing may prevent the attack.

They may also suffer from all the other brassica pests and diseases but the fact that they are harvested so quickly means that these problems rarely occur.

HOW MUCH TO GROW?

You will get about 100 radishes in one square metre. This shows that you should sow little and often and never one square metre at one time.

VARIETIES

- Short Top Forcing (excellent and very reliable variety, very uniform).
- Cherry Belle (scarlet globe and quick to mature).

ROCKET

Latin name: *Eruca vesicaria* and *Eruca selvatica*
Family: *Brassicaeae (*also known as *Cruciferae)*

Both the wild and salad rocket are fashionable amongst chefs and gardeners alike. If grown at the right time they are such easy and delicious salad vegetables.

TYPES OF ROCKET
Salad rocket or rucola (*E. vesicaria*)
This is the more common type of rocket which can grow fairly tall (1m) if you let it go to flower. Both the leaves and flowers are edible.

Wild rocket (*E. selvatica*)
This is a wild relative of the salad rocket. It's a much smaller plant with narrower leaves. Even if this plant bolts, you can simply cut it back to about 5cm above ground and it will re-grow again.

SOIL AND SITE

Rocket does well in any reasonably fertile soil.

SOWING

The best time to sow rocket is in early August until early October. I usually sow 5–7 seeds in modules. The modular transplants are ready for planting out about 4 weeks after sowing.

You can make more successional sowings from late January until April but they never perform as well as the autumn sown crops. They are likely to bolt prematurely and also get attacked by the fleabeetle.

SPACING

- Between rows: 25cm.
- Between plants: 20cm (5 plants per station).

PLANT CARE

It is essential to keep the plot completely weed-free and watered regularly.

HARVESTING

You can either harvest individual leaves as required or use the cut-and-come-again method: cut the whole plant at about 5cm height from the soil level and the leaves will re-grow. This procedure can be repeated within the next 2–3 weeks.

POTENTIAL PROBLEMS

Rocket is very prone to fleabeetle attacks. The symptoms are hundreds of minute holes in the leaves that are caused by a tiny shiny black beetle. The autumn and late winter sowings will escape the fleabeetle. If you are determined to grow rocket in spring and summer you will have to cover the beds as soon as they are planted with a fine netting such as fleece or a fine Enviromesh.

HOW MUCH TO GROW?

Rocket is a very prolific salad, so 3–4 plants (multi-seeded modules) should be sufficient especially if you also grow other winter salads.

VARIETIES

- Salad Rocket (large lobed leaves with excellent flavour).
- Salad Rocket Victoria (an improved rocket variety with a rounded leaf blade and attractive dark green colour).
- Salad Rocket Dentallata (an excellent variety of salad rocket with serrated leaves resembling wild rocket).
- Wild Rocket (small serrated leaves with intense flavour).
- Wild Rocket Napoli (an improved wild rocket with a more upright growth habit and a darker colour).

SCALLION OR SPRING ONION

Latin name: *Allium cepa*
Family: *Alliaceae* (commonly known as Alliums)

With the help of a polytunnel or greenhouse you can harvest scallions for nearly twelve months of the year. In order to achieve this you need to get into a routine and sow small quantities at regular intervals.

Scallions are grown for their small, white shanks and tender, green stem and leaves. They are also very easy and quick to grow.

SOIL AND SITE
Scallions prefer a pH of 6.5–7 and grow in any reasonably fertile soil.

SOWING
In order to get regular crops of freshly harvested scallions you need to sow them at regular intervals every second week starting from late January (on a heating bench) until early September.

I usually sow the seeds into modular trays, 10 seeds per cell and about 1.5cm deep. The trays are placed on a heated bench or on a warm, south-facing windowsill. About 4 weeks after sowing each module is planted out together as a bunch (without separating the seedlings). If they are planted like this they are a lot easier to maintain and harvest.

SPACING
I plant bunches of ten seedlings together at a spacing of 25 x 25cm.

PLANT CARE
Regular watering is essential as scallions prefer to grow in moist soil. If the soil is too dry they may develop a bulbous growth.

HARVESTING
Scallions are ready about 4–6 weeks after planting out. Harvesting is very easy if they are already growing in bunches. Simply pull or fork out the bunches, knock off some excess soil from the roots, cut off the tops so the bunches are about 30cm long and tie them together with a rubber band. Only harvest scallions as you need them as they will not keep well once they are harvested.

POTENTIAL PROBLEMS
Scallions may suffer from the same pests and diseases as onions but to a much lesser extent because they mature so much faster.

Downy mildew is the only problem I have encountered with scallions and only if I left the plants too long in the ground.

HOW MUCH TO GROW?
You will get 16 bunches of scallions per square metre.

VARIETIES

By far the two best varieties of scallions are:

- Parade (a high quality variety, very reliable and easy to grow, excellent flavour).
- Ishikura Bunching (a very vigorous growing single stalk variety, excellent for growing in tunnels and greenhouses all year round).

SHALLOT

Latin name: *Allium cepa* (Aggregatum Group
Family: *Alliaceae* (commonly known as Alliums)

Shallots are less popular than onions but some celebrity chefs try to encourage their use. They are easy to grow and have quite a distinctive flavour. They are also very interesting in that if you plant one bulb (set) it multiplies and forms a clump of about eight bulbs.

SOIL AND SITE
Shallots require the same soil and site condition as onions. The ideal soil pH ranges from 6.5–7.

PLANTING
Shallots are best grown from sets (small shallots) which can be planted from early February until March in a tunnel or greenhouse. Smaller sets are less likely to bolt than the larger ones. The sets should be planted so that the tip is still showing at the soil surface. It is essential to keep shallots in the allium section to minimize various soil-borne diseases such as white rot.

SPACING
- Between plants: 25cm.
- Between rows: 30cm.

PLANT CARE
Apart from weeding there is little else to do. You have to be careful when you hoe so that you do not damage the bulbs or disturb the roots. Hand weeding may be more appropriate at the later stages.

HARVESTING
Shallots are ready a few weeks before onions. They are ready when three quarters of the leaves have fallen down and turned yellow. The best way to dry the bulbs is to leave them on the beds, ideally not touching each other, in full sun. Pull or fork out the shallots on a sunny day and leave them outside until the first rains. Then move them into an open shed and lay them on chicken wire or pallets in a single layer. You want to keep the rain off but still have good air circulation. You should also remove excess soil around the roots but do not remove the skins.

STORING
If you manage to dry the bulbs sufficiently they will store in a cool, ventilated shed until March.

POTENTIAL PROBLEMS
Shallots suffer from the same pests and diseases as onions.

HOW MUCH TO GROW?
You will only need to plant a few shallots in a tunnel or greenhouse to get some shallots before the outdoor crop is ready in August.

VARIETIES

Unfortunately there is only a limited number of varieties available in garden centres. Just make sure the sets are of good quality.

If available try the following varieties:

- Red Sun (deep red brown skin, very early, excellent flavour).
- Golden Gourmet (yellow skin, firm even bulbs, stores well).

SPINACH, ANNUAL

Latin name: *Spinacia oleracea*
Family: *Chenopodiaceae* (Goosefoot Family)

Annual spinach is the real spinach. It is superior in taste compared to perpetual spinach. Unfortunately it is trickier to grow as it has a very short lifecycle and is prone to bolting. However with the use of a tunnel or greenhouse you can grow the most delicious annual spinach for about ten months of the year. It is an excellent vegetable for early spring and late autumn.

SOIL AND SITE
Spinach requires a rich, fertile soil with a pH value between 6.5 and 7.5. It will benefit from generous compost or composted manure applications.

SOWING AND PLANTING
In order to get a continuous supply of annual spinach you should sow seeds every 3–4 weeks from early February until mid

September. The early sowings (February to late April) and late sowings (August to September) should be planted in a tunnel or greenhouse whereas the other sowings (May to July) can be planted outdoors.

The early sowings in February and March should be sown in modular trays and placed on a heating bench at 18°C. I generally sow 4 seeds per cell and about 1.5cm deep. The seedlings are not divided when planted out about 4 weeks after. Later sowings can either be made into modular trays or direct into a well prepared fine seed bed.

SPACING
- Plant spacing: 7cm for baby-leaf spinach and 15cm for normal sized spinach.
- Row spacing: 25cm

For direct sown crops it is important to thin the seedlings early to the recommended spacing as this discourages bolting.

INTERCROPPING
Annual spinach is an excellent vegetable for intercropping. It is a neutral vegetable (not susceptible to any specific disease) and not related to the troublesome families such as the brassicas or alliums. Due to its short-lived nature and low growth habit, it can be used anywhere to fill a space quickly.

HARVESTING
You can harvest spinach at the baby leaf stage about 40 days after sowing and ordinary spinach is ready after about 50 days from sowing. Young spinach leaves make an excellent addition to a salad. Individual leaves can be harvested as required by twisting or cutting the outside leaves. It can also be used as a cut-and-come-again crop. Depending on the season, you can expect between two to five cuts

per plant. The very early and late summer crops are a lot less prone to bolting and thus you can get a much better and longer yield.

PLANT CARE
Never let the soil dry out especially during the propagation and early development stage. Water regularly during dry spells and keep the plot weed-free at all times.

POTENTIAL PROBLEMS
Slugs and aphids are the main pests. Downy mildew is the most common disease. The symptoms are white fluffy patches on the underside of the leaves. If most of the leaves are diseased it is better to remove the plants and start again. Some varieties are more resistant to the disease than others.

HOW MUCH TO GROW?
You will get about 40 plants per square metre. Grow half a square metre every 3 weeks.

VARIETIES
- Firebird F1 (a fantastic variety, high yielding, dark green and good resistance to mildew).
- Emilia F1 (versatile variety suitable for all year round production, mildew- and bolt-resistant).
- Galaxi F1 (very hardy variety, suitable for autumn, winter and spring cropping).
- Palco F1 (quick to establish and relatively slow to bolt, excellent resistance to mildew, suited to autumn and early spring sowings).
- Renegade F1 (an excellent variety for summer and autumn sowings, upright growth, mildew-resistant).
- Reddy F1 (unique variety with attractive dark red stems and veins, sow February to April, but prone to bolting).

SPINACH, PERPETUAL

Latin name: *Beta vulgaris* subsp. *flavescens*
Family: *Chenopodiaceae* (Goosefoot Family)

Perpetual spinach is also known as spinach beet or leaf beet. It must be one of the easiest vegetables to grow and, with the use of a tunnel or greenhouse, you can harvest it for ten months of the year. You can extend the growing season of perpetual spinach with a late August/early September sowing and you can start picking leaves from late October onwards.

During very cold spells the tops may die back but they will come back in late February and the plants will continue to produce leaves until April.

SOIL AND SITE

Perpetual spinach will do well in any fertile soil. It benefits greatly from generous manure applications prior to planting.

SOWING AND PLANTING

Perpetual spinach is very easy to establish. Seed should be sown into modular trays (one seed per cell) and then placed onto a heating bench at 18°C. You will notice that from the one seed about 3–5 seedlings appear. They are clusters of seeds. In order to get one good strong plant you need to thin out the seedlings to leave just the strongest one in each cell.

Two sowing dates are sufficient to get a continuous supply of perpetual spinach throughout autumn, winter and spring: late August and early January.

The seedlings can be planted about 5 weeks after sowing.

SPACING

- Between plants: 30cm.
- Between rows: 30cm.

PLANT CARE

Keep the crop weed-free and well watered especially during warm spells. It's also beneficial to remove the lower leaves which turn brown if not harvested on time.

HARVESTING

Harvest the leaves continually throughout the growing season by twisting them away from the base of the plant. It is a down, push, twist movement. Try it a few times to get practice. It is much better for the plant than cutting it and ending up with diseased little stumps.

HOW MUCH TO GROW?

You will get 5 plants per square metre. This is more than adequate for each sowing.

VARIETIES

- Perpetual Spinach (the most common variety).
- Erbette (light green, crinkly leaves).

Note Plant breeders have shown very little interest in this vegetable which reflects the absence of varieties. The one variety which is most available is simply called Perpetual Spinach, like the vegetable itself.

I have found massive variation of Perpetual Spinach from different seed companies. Some are much better than others.

SQUASH AND PUMPKIN

Latin name: *Cucurbita maxima, pepo* and *moschata*
Family: *Cucurbitaceae*

Squashes and pumpkins are one of the most vigorous vegetables. But be warned, they can very easily take over your whole greenhouse or polytunnel. They are a very bad choice for a small greenhouse. Some varieties can easily cover an area of 5–7 square metres, rambling over any neighbouring crop.

Both squashes and pumpkins grow extremely well outdoors especially if planting out is delayed until late May/early June.

The only types suitable for a tunnel or greenhouse are bush types. Alternatively you can train trailing varieties up strings and remove all side-shoots.

SOIL AND SITE

Squashes need a very fertile, free-draining soil which can hold plenty of moisture. A generous application of well-decomposed compost is beneficial. They also need a sunny location in the tunnel or greenhouse.

SOWING

Squashes and pumpkins are very tender plants. Any touch of frost will kill them. For growing indoors I usually sow the seeds in early April individually into 7cm pots. Ideally the pots are left in a propagator in the greenhouse or on the windowsill at home (south-facing). After about 3–4 weeks – or before the plants get pot bound – I pot them on into 12cm pots and leave them on the heating bench.

PLANTING

The plants can be planted out into the beds in the tunnel or greenhouse around mid May.

SPACING

- Bush varieties: 1m apart each way.
- Trailing varieties: 75cm apart if trained up strings.

PLANT CARE

Keep the plants weed-free, especially in the early stages as it will be very difficult later on to get to the weeds. If they are well weeded at the start the large leaves will prevent new seeds from germinating.

Both pumpkins and squashes will try to grow over neighbouring vegetables, so they need to be kept in check.

HAND POLLINATION

Early in the year you may have to help the plants with pollination. This will increase your chances of fruits.

Squash and pumpkins have separate male and female flowers. They are easily distinguishable by looking at the flower stalk. The male stalk is plain and the female flower carries a small fruit on its stalk.

You transfer the pollen from the male to the female flowers with a soft brush or remove the male flower and rub it onto the open blooms of the female flowers.

HARVESTING AND STORING

Summer squashes should be harvested every week. Some varieties such as Sunburst F1 are very prolific. If you let the fruit mature, the yield will be reduced.

Winter squashes are harvested in late autumn before the first frost. If you want to store squashes, leave the fruits to mature on the vine at least until October. The mature fruits have hard outer shells. Use a sharp knife to cut the stems (or handles) of the fruits to be stored and leave the stem attached to the fruit. If the leaves of the plants are still green that means that the fruit is not yet cured and will not store for long. You should then leave the fruits out in a sunny spot for about 10 days and only move them in if frost threatens. Then store in a dry, fairly cool place until March.

POTENTIAL PROBLEMS

Squash and pumpkin plants need to be protected from slugs in the early stages straight after planting out.

HOW MUCH TO GROW?

One or two plants are sufficient otherwise you will have no room left for anything else. And please heed my advice: don't let them take over!

VARIETIES

Summer squash
- Patty Pan (pale green scalloped-edged fruits, needs to be harvested regularly).
- Sunburst F1 (highly attractive and delicious bright yellow flat scalloped-edged fruits, very high yielding).

Winter squash
- Butternut F1 (the best known and one of the most delicious squashes but needs a good summer to do well in Ireland, trailing habit).

- Crown Prince F1 (one of the best flavoured squashes, steel grey skin and orange flesh, store well, trailing habit).
- Delicata – Cornell Strain (my favourite one for taste, also known as the sweet potato squash, cream colour with green stripes, needs a good summer to do well, bush habit).
- Sweet Dumpling (produces a large number of small fruits with striped skin and creamy white flesh, bush habit).
- Table Ace F1 (dark green acorn shaped fruits weighing up to 1 kg with a nutty flavour, trailing habit).
- Turk's Turban (turban shaped, highly decorative and edible fruit, very prolific and well suited to Irish conditions, trailing habit).
- Uchiki Kuri (orange/red pear-shaped fruit, nutty flavour).
- Vegetable Spaghetti (the fruit can be baked whole and the flesh can be scooped out – it looks like spaghetti).

STEVIA

Latin name: *Stevia rebaudiana*
Family: *Asteraceae*

Stevia is such an interesting and wonderful plant for the polytunnel and greenhouse. It is not a vegetable or a herb but it was proclaimed as one of the healthiest sugar substitutes and shortly afterwards was banned for commercial sugar production. Apparently the ban was due to health concern but many people are convinced it was because of commercial reasons.

Stevia leaves are about ten times higher in sugar than normal sugar. They are ideal for sweetening herbal teas. There are also claims that it can be used as an antibacterial agent and for regulating blood pressure as well as preventing tooth decay and colds.

Stevia is a tender perennial but I always grow it as an annual just like basil. You can try and bring cuttings of it through the winter in a conservatory.

SOIL AND SITE

Stevia is a tender perennial that prefers to grow in light sandy soils with a pH of 6.5–7. It requires full sun and should only be planted out when all danger of frost is past which is usually (but definitely not guaranteed) in late May or early June in a tunnel.

SOWING AND PROPAGATION

As it is a very tender plant I only start sowing it in late April. The seeds have a low germination rate so I usually sow about 10 seeds into a 9cm pot about 0.5cm deep. The pot is placed in a propagator at 20°C or a warm south-facing windowsill. The seeds will germinate after about 3 weeks. When the first true leaf appears (usually about 2 weeks after germination) the seedlings can be pricked out into individual small pots (7cm pots) using potting compost. The plants can be planted out into the greenhouse or tunnel border in early June.

You can also take cuttings from the plants during the end of the growing season. The best cuttings are heeled cuttings where you twist off a side-shoot (about 10cm long) with the heel still attached to it. About half to three quarters of all the leaves should be removed and the cuttings inserted at least half way into pots and then covered with a 'tent' of clear plastic for about a week. These cuttings are ideal for overwintering in a conservatory or warm and south-facing windowsill.

SPACING

- Between plants: 45cm.
- Between rows: 45cm.

PLANT CARE

During the summer stevia is a very easy plant to look after. All you need to do is to water and weed. Towards the end of the growing season the plants quickly deteriorate in an unheated greenhouse or polytunnel.

HARVESTING

The leaves can be harvested from late summer until late autumn. They can be used fresh or dried. Once the leaves are completely dry you should store them in an airtight container. Stevia should be harvested like basil. Instead of picking individual leaves you should cut the tips above a set of leaves.

VARIETIES

There are no known varieties of stevia while at the same time there is a massive difference in the sugar content between individual plants. The ideal would be to make your own selections by sowing more than you need and planting only the 'sweetest' and by taking cuttings only from prime specimens.

STRAWBERRY

Latin name: *Fragaria x ananassa*
Family: *Rosaceae*

Strawberries are a wonderful crop for the polytunnel or greenhouse but only if you treat them as annuals. There are few things nicer than the first strawberries of the year. The indoor strawberries are at least a month earlier than the outdoor crop. After they have finished cropping, the plants should be removed to make space for another vegetable. Have you ever wondered why strawberries are called strawberries? Because they were traditionally mulched with straw to keep the berries away from slugs and reduce the risk of them rotting away when in contact with wet soil. Strawberries are one of the few fruits that carry the seeds on the outside. Nearly all other fruits enclose the seeds with their flesh.

SOIL AND SITE
Strawberries require a reasonably fertile soil. The plants will benefit from an application of well-decomposed compost prior to planting.

As soon as the plants begin to flower a light top-dressing of organic poultry pellets is beneficial.

PROPAGATION

Take runners from a healthy one-year-old strawberry plant in July/August. Fill a 9cm pot with potting compost and peg the first runners (little baby plants) into the pot using a piece of plain wire bent as a peg.

The stalks of the runners can be cut as soon as the new plant has started to root in the pot. At the end of August or early September the plants should be potted on into 15cm pots and left outside in the coldest spot in your garden until the end of January. They require a cold spell to initiate flowering.

PLANTING

In late January or early February the plants can be planted into the polytunnel or greenhouse. They can be planted directly into the soil or alternatively into large pots, growbags (5 plants per growbag) or specially made wooden containers.

SPACING

- Between plants: 35cm.
- Between rows 35cm.

PLANT CARE

The plants should be kept moist but be careful not to water too much or there is a danger of encouraging fungal diseases. Strawberries can be planted through a mulch of Mypex which is a weed-suppressant material that allows water and air to penetrate and also keeps the fruits dry.

Alternatively you can use the traditional technique of mulching with straw. Good ventilation of the greenhouse is essential.

HARVESTING

Strawberries grown with protection will be ready much earlier than outdoor types. In fact they may be nearly finished by the time the outdoor crop is starting to produce fruit. The first harvest will be in early April and will last for about 4–6 weeks.

When they have finished producing, you should pull up the plants and compost them as they would produce a lot less the following year and take up valuable growing space during their non-productive period.

POTENTIAL PROBLEMS

The main problems with strawberries are grey mould and birds. To prevent grey mould you should ensure that the soil is well mulched so that the fruit is not resting on wet soil. Good ventilation and watering in the mornings or daytime instead of evening will also help to prevent grey mould. Birds are more a problem with your outdoor strawberries but if they also attack your indoor crop you should place anti-bird netting over the plants.

VARIETIES

- Gorella (probably the best variety for early tunnel or greenhouse production).

SWEET POTATO

Latin name: *Ipomea batatas*
Family: *Convolvulaceae*

Sweet potatoes may appear similar to our own potato, but they are really quite different. The potato belongs to the Nightshade family whereas the sweet potato belongs to the Convolvulus family. One well-known native member of the Convolvolus family is the common bindweed. The sweet potato is, like the common potato, a native of South America. From there it reached Polynesia before 1250 and New Zealand by the fourteenth century. How it got there is still unexplained. It was grown in Europe from the sixteenth century onwards. In fact, the Spanish introduced it into Europe long before the common potato. The early references of potatoes, including Shakespeare's were actually to sweet potatoes. In central and northern Europe it can only be grown with protection.

In the last decade the sweet potato has received a massive revival in popularity. Very few gardeners have been cultivating this vegetable but the breeding of 'Beauregard', a new variety which is less sensitive to day length, is changing this situation. There are slips (cuttings) from this variety available from many mail-order seed catalogues. It is impossible to grow successfully from tubers that are bought from a grocer.

SOIL AND SITE
Sweet potatoes thrive in a tropical climate which can only be achieved in your polytunnel or greenhouse. They require similar conditions to melons. The soil should be fertile and free-draining. A generous application of well-decomposed compost or manure is very beneficial. The ideal pH is 6.0. Ensure that sweet potatoes are growing on the sunny side of the greenhouse.

SOWING AND PROPAGATION
When you start growing sweet potatoes you should order 'slips' from a mail order seed company. You should receive the slips around late April/early May. As soon as they arrive you should pot them on individually into 9cm pots and place the pots on a heating bench or on a warm south-facing windowsill. The plants can be planted out into the polytunnel or greenhouse in early June. In the following years you can reserve some tubers to get good cutting material. In early April you should put some tubers in a single layer into a large pot filled with moist sand and place them on the heating bench or warm windowsill. After a few weeks you'll notice shoots appearing and when the shoots are about 10–15cm long they should be cut just below a leaf joint. Remove the lower leaves and plant the cuttings individually into 9cm pots containing free-draining compost. You can place a clear plastic bag over the cuttings to prevent moisture loss. Remove the bag after a few days. Each tuber will produce about 7 cuttings.

They can be planted into the greenhouse soil once a good root system has developed and before the plants become pot-bound.

SPACING
- Between plants: 30cm.
- Between rows: 75cm.

PLANT CARE
The plants should be kept moist while they are actively growing and should be watered two to three times per week. Later on in the year they require a drier soil so the tubers will ripen. Watering once a week will be sufficient.

Tubers are produced fastest when the day length is longer than 14 hours. Unfortunately in our climate this is not the case in autumn when they should mature. But luckily, as mentioned above, there is now a variety ('Beauregard') available that is less sensitive to day length.

From mid July onwards the plants would benefit from a weekly comfrey liquid application.

The sweet potato leaves are twining vines and are rather unruly trailing all over the place. They can be pruned gently to encourage branching out. You can also let them climb up bamboo canes or strings.

HARVESTING
The tubers are ready to harvest in autumn when the leaves have turned yellow. They should be dug out carefully. They will keep well in a plastic bag in the fridge or stored in moist sand in a cool but frost-free shed.

POTENTIAL PROBLEMS
Sweet potatoes are susceptible to whitefly and red spider mite. To avoid these you should mist the plants regularly and spray with a garlic and nettle spray.

VARIETIES
Beauregard is the only daylength sensitive variety available at present, but I'm sure more varieties will become available in the near future.

SWEETCORN

Latin name: *Zea mays*
Family: *Gramineae*

There is no comparison between eating a freshly harvested sweetcorn and a shop bought one. The reason for this is that once the cob has been harvested the sugar is steadily converted into starch. A tunnel or greenhouse will provide ideal growing conditions for this delicious vegetable. Unfortunately it is a very low yielding plant, producing only two cobs per plant. Commercially it would be foolish to produce sweetcorn in a tunnel but for the hobby gardener and hobby gourmet there are few experiences more memorable than growing and eating your own sweetcorn.

SOIL AND SITE
Sweetcorn requires a fertile, free-draining, but moisture retentive soil. A generous application of well-rotted compost is essential.

Ensure that the growing crop is not shaded by another tall vegetable such as tomatoes or cucumbers.

SOWING

You can sow individual seeds in small pots (7cm) about 2.5cm deep in mid April. The pots should be placed on a heating bench at 18–20°C. About 5 weeks later they can be planted.

SPACING

- Between plants: 45cm.
- Between rows: 45cm.

PLANT CARE

Sweetcorn is the only vegetable in the Gramineae family and there is no risk of any soil-borne pest or disease affecting it. So really you can plant it wherever it suits you.

Sweetcorn should be planted in rectangular blocks as opposed to single lines. This will ensure successful pollination. The male flowers are on top of the plant and the female flowers are the tassels at the end of the cobs. Each little silky strand has to receive a pollen grain to develop a kernel. You may have noticed some kernels missing from a cob. They didn't get pollinated. In a tunnel or greenhouse where there is no wind you have to do the job of pollination. When the pollen is ready you have to shake the plants every day so that the pollen lands on the tassels.

HARVESTING

In late summer you should check regularly to see if the tassels at the end of the cobs wither and turn brown. When this happens double check if the cob is ripe by carefully peeling off part of the sheath. You then squeeze a kernel and if a milky juice comes out it's ready to harvest. If it is clear liquid you have to wait a bit longer.

POTENTIAL PROBLEMS
Generally sweetcorn grows very healthily in a tunnel and the only problem you may encounter is poor pollination.

VARIETIES
There is a staggering range of sweetcorn available ranging from the traditional types to the sweet and super sweet varieties

Traditional varieties
• Black Aztec (kernels are blue black, can be eaten fresh or dried).
• Golden Bantam (very good quality, sweet flavour).

Supersweet varieties
• Sweet Nugget F1 (excellent yield of long, uniform cobs).
• Swift F1 (one of the best flavoured sweetcorn, exceptionally sweet and succulent kernels).

SWISS CHARD

Latin name: *Beta vulgaris* subsp. *cicla*
Family: *Chenopodiaceae* (Goosefoot Family)

Swiss Chard is also known as silver chard, silver beet and seakale beet. There are other types: Ruby Chard with red stems and red-veined leaves, Rainbow Chard with multi-coloured stems and leaves and also recently introduced a Yellow Chard with yellow stems and veins. They are all very decorative as well as tasty crops.

All chards are excellent crops for winter cropping in a tunnel or greenhouse.

SOIL AND SITE
Chard will do well in any fertile soil provided that plenty of compost or composted manure has been applied. The ideal soil pH is 6.5–7.5.

SOWING AND PLANTING
Seed can be sown into modular trays (one seed per cell) and placed onto a heating bench at 18°C. As with perpetual spinach and

beetroot you will notice that from the one seed about three to five seedlings appear. You have to thin them out as soon as they appear, leaving just one seedling per module.

Two strategic sowing dates in late August and in early January are sufficient to get a continuous supply of chard throughout autumn, winter and spring.

SPACING
- Between plants: 35cm.
- Between rows: 35cm.

PLANT CARE
Keep the crop weed-free and well watered at all times. It is also beneficial to remove the lower leaves which turn brown if not harvested on time.

HARVESTING
Just like perpetual spinach, harvest the leaves on a regular basis by twisting them away from the base of the plant.

HOW MUCH TO GROW?
Three plants for each sowing will provide you with a lot of chard. This will take up less than one square metre from each sowing.

VARIETIES
- Swiss Chard (long, thick white stems and dark green leaves).
- Rhubarb Chard (red stemmed version of Swiss chard).
- Rainbow Chard (mixture of various coloured stems and leaves, very ornamental).

TOMATO

Latin name: *Lycopersicon esculentum*
Family: *Solanaceae* (Nightshade Family)

The name '*Lycopersicon*' derives from the Greek, '*lycos*', a wolf, and '*persicon*', a peach, probably in reference to its supposed poisonous qualities. '*Esculentum*' however means edible.

Tomatoes are certainly one of the most exciting tunnel and greenhouse vegetables to grow. The flavour of home-grown tomatoes can never be matched by the bland and thick skinned supermarket ones. In fact, modern tomatoes are bred so that they will last for weeks on supermarket shelves and don't bruise when handled. The other trouble is that they are grown without soil often in straw-bale culture that is drenched with artificial fertilizers and with supplementary heat and lighting.

They are nearly as badly treated as battery farmed hens.

HISTORY

The tomato grows wild in South America. It was first cultivated in Mexico by American Indians and brought back to Spain by Spanish Conquistadores. In 1544 it reached Italy. Soon after it spread throughout Europe. It took a long time for the tomato to turn from a pretty ornamental plant into a vegetable.

SOIL AND SITE

Tomatoes require a very fertile soil. Just imagine a full sized tomato plant – well over two metres tall and all the hundreds of fruits it produces. It needs a lot of nutrients. The best feed is composted farmyard manure or garden compost. I usually incorporate a full wheelbarrow composted manure into the soil for every three square metres.

If they are grown in pots or growbags, ensure that the pots are large enough (40 litres) and that you don't plant more than two plants per growbag. I have to admit I'm not a fan of growing tomatoes in growbags or pots as their growing space is far too restricted. Obviously if you haven't got a suitable spot in your border, growbags may be the only option.

SOWING

Tomatoes need to be raised on a heating bench or warm south-facing windowsill. Best results are achieved when the temperature is set on 21°C. Seeds are best sown in late February until mid March into traditional open seed trays (not modular trays). Seeds should be sown thinly into the trays (about 100 seeds per standard tray) or pots (about 10 seeds per 9cm pot). Then the seeds should be covered lightly with seed compost using a sieve and pressed in using a wooden board that fits snugly into the tray.

Keep the trays moist at all times – never overwater them or let them dry out. The tomato seedlings should emerge after 10 days. It is very important to prick out the seedlings as early as possible, ideally into 10cm pots containing a richer potting compost.

Remember to hold the seedlings by the seed leaves (cotyledons) and plant the seedlings so the seed leaves are just above soil level. During this stage the plants should remain on the heating bench. Young plants in pots must be spaced out as soon as their leaves are touching – roughly about every 3 weeks. If you fail to do this, the plants will become weak and spindly.

PLANTING

When the plants are well rooted in their pots and before they get pot bound, they can be planted. The best time is in May. Tomato plants can be trained up strings that are attached to an overhead wire. After digging the planting hole, lay the bottom part of the string into the hole and tie the other end to the overhead wire. Plant the tomato plant on top of the string and cover and gently firm the soil around the plant to leave no air pocket around it. If your tomato plants have become leggy you can plant them deeper. This will strengthen the plants.

SPACING

The plants should be spaced out 50cm apart. You can have a single or double row per bed. The yield is obviously higher from a double row but a single row usually produces healthier plants.

PLANT CARE
Side-shooting

Every week you have to side-shoot your plants. Many beginners find it difficult to distinguish between a normal leaf, a side-shoot, a flower truss and the main stem. Just remember that the side-shoot is the one between the main stem and a leaf, always the one in the middle.

Fig. 9. Side-shooting tomatoes.

No matter how long the side-shoots have become and even if they already have flowers on them, you have to remove them. When the side-shoots are small you can nip them off with your fingers, but when bigger you need to use a sharp knife or secateurs. The other weekly job is to wind the growing plants around the twine and remove the lower leaves that start to turn yellow.

HARVESTING

You can expect your first harvest of tomatoes in July, possibly slightly earlier in very warm parts. My favourite variety 'Sungold F1' is always the first one to ripen and often the one that lasts longest. It is also high yielding. You will often get up to 400 most delicious cherry tomatoes from it.

It is important to harvest your tomatoes regularly – at least once a week – otherwise the fruit becomes over-ripe and rots or splits. You can expect to get a regular supply of tomatoes until the end of October and, in some years, right into November.

POTENTIAL PROBLEMS

Unfortunately tomatoes can be affected by a whole range of pests, diseases and disorders.

Fruit splitting

This is quite common with tomatoes. It is caused through irregular watering and a sudden burst of growth occurs after a dry period. Some varieties of tomato are more prone to splitting than others. A regular watering regime may solve this problem.

Blossom end rot

The symptom of blossom end rot is a dark and often rotting area at the base of the tomato fruits. This disorder is caused by a shortage of calcium. Often the calcium is not absorbed quickly enough due to a lack of water.

Greenback

The symptoms of greenback are hard unripe green patches on the fruit while the rest of the fruit is fully ripe. Hot conditions can cause this uneven ripening. In order to prevent greenback, ensure that there is adequate ventilation and in warmer areas consider shading your tunnel or greenhouse during the summer months.

Greenhouse whitefly

This little white aphid also affects peppers and aubergines. As it originates from Mexico it cannot survive outdoors. The symptoms are sticky leaves that in turn get infected by sooty mould and then turn black. You will also see the small white flies that take to the air when the plant is disturbed. The whitefly is mostly found on the underside of the lower leaves.

There is an easy way to never get whitefly into your tunnel or greenhouse. You simply raise all your tomatoes, peppers and aubergines from seed. The only way of getting whitefly in the first place is from affected plants.

Most gardeners who have had a tunnel or greenhouse for many years will probably already have them. There is now a very effective control and this is the *Encarsia formosa* – a biological control. It is a tiny parasitic wasp that feeds on the whitefly. You can buy the eggs of the wasp by mail order. The timing is important. They should be released as soon as the first whitefly appear. If there is already an infestation it's too late. It is so successful and reliable that now even conventional tomato growers prefer this method to chemical control.

Grey mould (Botrytis)

Grey mould is a very common disease in tunnels and greenhouses. It affects many different and unrelated vegetables. Tomatoes are usually affected from late summer/early autumn onwards when it becomes more damp and cool. The symptoms are grey fluffy moulds on leaves, stems or fruit. As a prevention, provide the best possible ventilation even on wet days. You don't want condensation to build up on the plastic or polythene. Keep your tunnel or greenhouse tidy and remove any affected leaves and dispose of them.

If the disease is already on the stem you can try the milk and water spray. You use one part milk to 5 parts water and spray the mix on three consecutive days onto the affected part of the stem and you'll find that the disease stops spreading.

Blight

Both potatoes and tomatoes can suffer from potato blight. It's not often a problem in tunnels and greenhouses but in bad years it can quickly wipe out your tomato crop. There is no cure for it but there is now a blight-resistant tomato variety available – Ferline F1 – and it even tastes quite nice.

Magnesium deficiency

The symptom is yellowing of the leaves while the leaf veins remain green. The older leaves are affected first. If your soil is deficient in magnesium you can use magnesium limestone. If you live near a quarry, you can ask which type they have. It is usually quite inexpensive to buy ground limestone.

HOW MUCH TO GROW?

Six good tomato plants are enough if you just want to eat a few tomatoes every day from July until October.

If you want to preserve tomatoes for the winter you can grow about 15 to 20 plants.

VARIETIES

- Beefsteak (large fleshy fruit weighing up to 500g. Vigorous growing indeterminate type).
- Brandywine (a delicious but quite low yielding heritage variety).
- Marmande (a large tomato with uneven shaped fruits and lots of flavour, not a high yielder).
- Rosada F1 (a cherry plum with excellent flavour, indeterminate type).
- Sungold F1 (my favourite tomato of all with the nicest flavour and high yield of golden orange cherry tomatoes. Start cropping very early and lasts longest, very hard to beat!).
- Shirley F1 (a good normal sized tomato, very reliable and high yielding variety, indeterminate type).
- Tigerella (a most unusual variety with striped fruits, one of the best for taste, indeterminate type).
- Tumbler F1 (an extra early bush variety for hanging baskets or pots. The plant has a cascading habit with bright red cherry fruits of excellent flavour. Do not side-shoot!).

TURNIP

Latin name: *Brassica napus* (Rapifera Group)
Family: *Brassicaceae* (also known as *Cruciferae*)

Turnips are such rewarding quick growing vegetables, the only shame is that they are not very popular. They are also often confused with swedes. Turnip roots may be flat, round or elongated; the flesh is mostly white and sometimes yellow. Swedes are larger, have a yellow flesh and often a purple top.

A polytunnel or greenhouse can extend the growing season of turnip by at least two months especially early in the season.

SOIL AND SITE
Turnips will grow in a range of soils provided they are reasonably fertile. Compost application is highly beneficial. The ideal pH is 6.8.

SOWING AND PLANTING

Turnip seeds can either be sown directly into the soil or in modular trays which are placed on a heating bench at 15–18°C in a tunnel or greenhouse. I sow one or two seeds per module about 1.5cm deep. If two seeds germinate you have to remove the weaker seedling. They usually germinate within 5–7 days and are ready for planting out about 3 weeks after sowing.

You can make the first sowing in late January and then again in late February and late March. Any later sowing will do better outdoors.

SPACING

- Between plants: 15cm (or 10cm if you want to harvest the thinnings).
- Between rows: 25cm.

ROTATION

It is essential to keep turnips in the brassica section of your rotation to prevent a build up of the numerous brassica pests and diseases.

PLANT CARE

Keep well weeded and water during dry spells.

HARVESTING AND STORAGE

Baby turnips can be harvested when the roots are about 5cm in diameter. Instead of the recommended 15cm spacing between plants you could space them 10cm apart and harvest every second root while it is still small. Turnips should always be eaten fresh. They are not as well suited for long term storage as swedes.

POTENTIAL PROBLEMS

Turnips are susceptible to all the brassica troubles and, as with the swede, fleabeetles cause most havoc later in the season. The first sowings in the tunnel or greenhouse should avoid the attacks.

HOW MUCH TO GROW?
You should get 24 turnips per square metre.

VARIETIES
- Market Express F1 (pure white early Japanese type, cold tolerant).
- Milan Purple Top (very reliable variety with purple tops and a white base).
- Oasis (very unusual melon flavoured variety).
- Snowball (small quick growing variety with white skin).
- White Globe (smooth round roots of white flesh with bright purple tops).

YACON

Latin name: *Polymnia sonchifolia* or *Smallanthus sonchifolium*
Family: *Compositae*

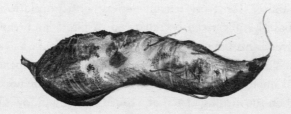

Yacon is really one of my favourite vegetables to grow. It originates in the Andes and was one of the Inca vegetables. It is closely related to the dahlia and produces large edible tubers that even resemble dahlia tubers. In a tunnel or greenhouse it can grow into a large plant and produces a very high yield of sweet tasting tubers that can be eaten raw or cooked. It could become one of the new superfoods as its carbohydrates are not stored as starch but as inulin and could thus play an important part in a diabetic's diet. The reason is that it is not absorbed from the gut and therefore does not raise the blood sugar. Apparently yacon leaves were used by the Incas as toilet paper.

SOIL AND SITE
Yacon requires a free-draining, fertile and well balanced soil and should be grown in full sun.

SOWING AND PLANTING
Yacon can only be grown from stem tubers. The problem is that they are difficult to obtain so you need to shop around. A good

source for finding anything less common is the publication: *The Plant Finder*.

Yacon plants have two types of tubers – very knobbly ones that cluster around the stalk and beautiful, large, smooth and succulent tubers that grow outside of the knobbly ones. Obviously the smooth succulent ones are for eating and the knobbly ones for propagation.

The knobbly tubers can be separated in late March/early April and, provided that they have a growth point, will make a new plant. Each part should be potted on into a 1 or 2 litre pot depending on the size of the tuber, using good potting compost. The pots should be placed on the heating bench or a south-facing window sill in the house. The plants can be planted into the tunnel or greenhouse around mid May.

SPACING
The plants grow huge with a spread similar to a courgette plant and a height of about 1.5 to 2 metres.
• Between plants: 1 metre

PLANT CARE
Apart from regular watering there is no additional maintenance required.

HARVESTING AND STORING
You should leave the plants in the ground until the first frost has killed the leaves. The tubers seem to grow a lot during the end of the season so the later the first frost, the higher the yield. The yield of tubers can be truly phenomenal and no other vegetable can match it. In one year I got 8 tubers each weighing nearly a pound.

Carefully dig out the whole plant and remove the smooth succulent tubers and use them immediately or store them in moist sand in a frost-free shed. What is left is the knobbly part of the plant. Store that in a bucket of moist sand in a frost-free shed. This can be split up in the following spring and you can give some new plants to your friends.

USES

The tubers are delicious raw and cooked. When eaten raw they have a surprisingly sweet taste. When cooked they remain crunchy and can be used as a potato alternative. They are also delicious roasted.

POTENTIAL PROBLEMS

One of the advantages of 'new' vegetables is that they are often free of any specific pests and diseases (the potato was grown for centuries in Europe without blight!). Apart from the occasional slug nibble on the leaves they grow completely healthy.

VARIETIES

There are no varieties of yacon.

CHOOSING A SITE

To locate the best site for your polytunnel or greenhouse, you need to consider the following. Obviously you may have to compromise to adjust to your own circumstances. The two most important considerations are good light and shelter from strong winds.

SHELTER
It is essential to choose a relatively sheltered spot for your polytunnel or greenhouse. You don't want to worry during every storm or gale about your tunnel blowing away or your glass panes breaking. A windbreak will provide adequate protection. The best windbreak is a natural hedge. Artificial windbreak netting also works well.

GOOD LIGHT - ASPECT
Good light levels are essential for healthy plant growth especially from autumn until spring. Position your greenhouse or polytunnel in order to get maximum sunshine throughout the year.

Ideally align your greenhouse or polytunnel in a north-south direction so you won't get any shading from tall crops that grow in the centre bed. Don't site your polytunnel or greenhouse next to buildings and trees as they will shade it and the roots of trees may grow into them.

ACCESS
The closer the greenhouse or polytunnel is to your house, the handier it is for you. They both require daily maintenance especially ventilation and watering. If you have a very pretty wooden or Victorian greenhouse you'll probably want to make it a central feature in your garden. If you have bought a polytunnel and are not too pleased with the aesthetics of it, you may want to screen it a little bit.

FROST POCKETS

If possible avoid low-lying areas in your garden where cold air accumulates otherwise there will be a danger of frost damage.

ACCESS TO WATER

A reliable source of water is crucial for the success of your greenhouse. Rainwater collection from the greenhouse roof is a great addition but rarely enough unless you have plenty of barrels to fill. A good source of mains water nearby may prove essential. In a polytunnel it is either very difficult or impossible to collect the rainwater so mains water is vital.

ELECTRICITY

A safe electricity power point inside the greenhouse or polytunnel is highly beneficial. It is necessary for heated propagators and you may also choose to have a light bulb in case you want to go on a slug hunt. You can also use it during early winter evenings. But other than that it is not essential.

PLANNING PERMISSION

If you are worried about planning regulations ask at your local council whether you need planning permission for a polytunnel or greenhouse.

CHOOSING A GREENHOUSE OR POLYTUNNEL

The choice between a polytunnel and a greenhouse is really quite simple. A greenhouse (also referred to as a glasshouse) is more expensive but more attractive than a polytunnel. However, if you have the skills to build your own greenhouse – even using recycled material (used windows or door frames) you could build it for next to nothing. Greenhouses are also slightly better in terms of heat retention and light transmission. Polytunnels, on the other hand, have really boomed in the last decade. They are relatively cheap and can be erected quite easily.

Fig. 10. Wooden greenhouse with red brick.

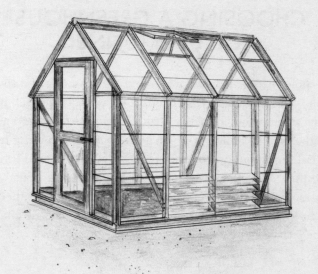

Fig. 11. Aluminium-framed greenhouse.

Fig. 12. Lean-to greenhouse.

Fig. 13. Polytunnel.

There are various aspects you should consider before purchasing either a polytunnel or greenhouse:

DOOR WIDTH AND HEIGHT
Ensure that you have a door on each side of the structure and make sure that it is as big as possible. In organic protected cropping, ventilation is the most important preventative measure for controlling fungal diseases.

ADEQUATE HEIGHT AND HEADROOM
Please don't buy a tiny claustrophobic polytunnel or greenhouse in which you have to dare yourself to go in. A taller structure is more beneficial for yourself and your plants.

QUALITY OF MATERIALS
Often – but not always – you pay more for a better material. Some tunnel or greenhouse manufacturers may be more expensive than others because they use better materials.

ADEQUATE PROVISION OF VENTILATION

As mentioned earlier, proper ventilation is crucial. Anybody who has been in a greenhouse or polytunnel when the sun shines knows about it. Have you ever thought where the term 'Greenhouse Effect' comes from?

CROP SUPPORTS

Crop supports are horizontal bars above head height. They allow you to train climbing plants, such as cucumbers, climbing beans and tomatoes, up a string that is attached to an overhead wire.

COVERS

There are a number of polythene covers available. Always opt for the slightly more expensive one that will hopefully last longer and have better light transmission and possibly even heat retention at night. A good cover that has been properly put on and is very tight should last about 5–7 years. It is important to wash the plastic every year, otherwise the light transmission can be significantly reduced and your plants will become leggy and more prone to disease.

For a greenhouse, glass is the traditional material. There is special horticultural glass available which is of very good quality.

There are also various types of plastic sheeting available, usually polythene (polyethylene), clear PVC and also polypropylene. Plastic sheeting has the advantage that it is doesn't break and shatter. Its disadvantage is its limited lifespan as it is affected by ultra-violet light. This will weaken it over time and may split the sheets.

USING A GREENHOUSE
OR POLYTUNNEL

Indoor space is valuable space, so you should try and make the most out of it. It is possible to get 5–6 crops per year from it as opposed to just one or two from outdoors.

To illustrate this here is a possible cropping schedule:

- **Late January**

  Plant early chitted potatoes.
- **April/May**

  Harvest potatoes, plant lettuce and scallions.
- **June**

  Harvest lettuce and scallions, plant celery.
- **August**

  Harvest celery, plant annual spinach.
- **September**

  Harvest annual spinach, plant oriental salads.

In order to achieve the above, you have to raise all the plants in modular trays. This will gain you about 4–8 weeks per crop.

GROWING METHODS

I always prefer growing vegetables in beds with improved soil. Growing in growbags or pots can be very restrictive to plant roots and you'll be forever watering and feeding the plants. If you have an extremely poor and wet soil you can consider putting up raised beds but be aware that then you have to water a lot more frequently.

PROPAGATION SPACE

A greenhouse or tunnel is an invaluable asset for your outdoor vegetable patch as you can finally liberate your house and windowsills and have a dedicated area for plant raising.

TO COMPLEMENT YOUR VEGETABLE GARDEN

The further north you live the shorter the growing season will be. A tunnel or greenhouse will give you the opportunity to prolong or nearly double the growing season of all vegetables. Indoors you can get courgettes for six months instead of three months outdoors, and salad can be harvested all year round if you choose the right varieties.

TO GROW WARM LOVING VEGETABLES

Many vegetables can't be grown successfully outdoors as they require a lot more heat and a lot less wind. It's nearly worth putting up a tunnel or greenhouse so you can grow your own tomatoes and cucumbers. The trouble is that the flavour of home-grown tomatoes can never be matched by supermarket tomatoes and you'll find it hard getting back to the bland shop ones in winter.

FOR LEISURE

As I mentioned in the Introduction, I have a friend who has a comfortable armchair and a little table with a radio in his greenhouse and he reckons it's the best escape of all. We had our wedding party in our greenhouse. Unfortunately a few tomato plants had to give way for the occasion.

Fig. 14. Sample layout of greenhouse or tunnel beds

MANAGING A GREENHOUSE OR POLYTUNNEL

WATERING

It is essential to have an adequate and reliable supply of water for your polytunnel or greenhouse. Rainwater can easily be collected from a greenhouse but not from a polytunnel. Rainwater is an excellent source of water but in many instances not sufficient so a nearby mains water supply is needed. Correct watering is necessary for successful indoor growing. It's an important skill every gardener will develop.

Common sense will go a long way. The soil should be kept moist – not too dry and not too wet. I think most beginners tend to over-water their tunnels or greenhouses. This is just as harmful as under-watering. If a soil is saturated with water there is very little air in the soil and the plants start to 'suffocate' and are unable to absorb nutrients.

There are various different watering systems available ranging from watering cans to an overhead sprinkler system.

HAND WATERING

This is by far my preferred method for a small greenhouse or polytunnel. The ideal method is to place a water barrel inside the greenhouse or tunnel – one at each end if the tunnel is big – and use watering cans with a good rose to water the plants. The advantage of the barrel being inside the tunnel is that the water has the same temperature as the plants. Plants often get a shock if the water is too cold. This applies especially to cucumbers. This way you can treat each vegetable according to its needs. Water basil very little. Don't get tomato and pepper leaves wet. Wet the leaves of cucumbers ideally with warm water to avoid cucumber mosaic virus and red spider mite.

Watering with watering cans can also keep us fit and the trip to the gym may become unnecessary. If you are in a meditative mode though you can simply use a hose pipe with a good fine spray lance.

DRIP AND TRICKLE IRRIGATION

There are a few systems available. A common one is the 'seep hose' that is made out of recycled car tyres. Other ones are called drip or trickle irrigation systems. With a seep hose the water 'seeps' out from the pores of the pipe. With the drip system the pipes release drops of water at regular intervals along the pipe.

Fig. 15. Drip irrigation.

The pipes are laid on the surface of the beds (one or two per bed) and are connected to a mains water supply. This system is well suited if you have low water pressure. If you want to be very lazy (or go away a lot) you can install a timer between the tap and the pipe and the water will come on automatically whenever you want.

It's a great idea but I still prefer to water the plants myself as I can observe and inspect them as I water. With this system it is also impossible to give some plants more than others. I think the biggest problem with drip irrigation is that people over-water as it is very difficult to guess how long to leave it on.

OVERHEAD SPRINKLER SYSTEM

An overhead sprinkler system is useful only for bigger greenhouses and polytunnels. The normal water pressure is rarely sufficient to run it so you need to get it checked before purchasing the system. I have met at least two people who bought it for their polytunnels only to discover that it doesn't work. If your water pressure is too low you need to get a large water tank and a pump.

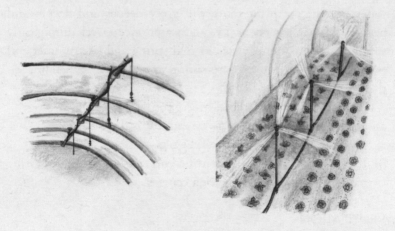

Fig. 16. Overhead sprinkler system.   *Fig. 17. Individual rotating sprinklers.*

SPRINKLERS

For a small tunnel or greenhouse one or two individual sprinklers are sufficient and normal water pressure can cope with it. The sprinklers are attached to a base about 60cm high and a normal hose pipe connects to it.

WHEN AND HOW OFTEN SHOULD I WATER?

Ideally you should water your greenhouse or polytunnel in the morning or afternoon. Watering in late evening especially during cold spells will increase the risk of fungal diseases spreading throughout your plants. Your plants should be dry before nightfall.

As a very general rule it is better to water infrequently and heavy. Frequent light watering will cause the roots of vegetables to grow more on the soil surface. When you water a dry soil make sure that the water is fully penetrating the soil. I usually water soil lightly and go over it a few times afterwards. An easy test is to scrape away the top inch of the soil and if it is still dry, water again and again. If you water heavily, the plant roots will grow deeper and deeper and become more independent. I would water once a week during early spring and late autumn, twice in mid spring and late summer and two or three times during late spring and summer depending on the weather.

Here are some tests to find out if your soil needs watering:

a) Scrape an inch of topsoil away and if it is dry beneath you have to water, if not the plants will be okay.

b) If you want to be more scientific you can buy moisture-testing meters from most good garden centres.

VENTILATION

Good ventilation is essential for healthy plant growth in your greenhouse or polytunnel. During the day the temperature can easily soar to well over 30°C when the sun shines even if there is a cool breeze outside. On the other hand, during night time the indoor temperature is not much different from the outside temperature. So it is an extreme micro-climate. It's important for a gardener to balance it to some extent by opening and closing the doors, vents or windows.

Most tunnel crops prefer warm temperatures at around 24–28°C. Temperatures over 30°C can slow down plant growth. Good ventilation can lessen the massive fluctuation between day and night temperature.

Another very important reason for having good ventilation is to avoid the spread of many fungal diseases that may attack your crops. If you are an organic gardener the only available option you have to control diseases is to prevent them in the first place. Fungal diseases such as grey mould (botrytis) and many others thrive in damp conditions with stagnant air.

Greenhouse
Make sure that your greenhouse has enough windows and vents and open them whenever possible. Roof windows are more efficient for cooling a greenhouse as hot air rises up. You can also buy automatic openers for the roof windows. These respond to temperature changes and are a worthwhile investment especially if you are out at work. Be careful though if it is too windy.

Polytunnel
When you buy a polytunnel make sure that the doors are as big as possible as they are often the only means of ventilation. One of the best tunnels is one with side ventilation. The lower section of the cover consists of strong green windbreak netting that is attached to the hoops on a wooden or aluminium rail about one metre above ground level. The polythene cover can be raised and lowered to cover the netting using a simple winding mechanism. You'll find that you get much stronger and healthier plants with side ventilation.

On larger tunnels you can also get overhead ventilation. Instead of one large sheet of polythene there are a few sheets and the overlap at the ridge can be opened and closed using the same winding mechanism as with the side ventilation. Any greenhouse and polytunnel manufacturer should be able to advise you on what would suit your needs best.

SHADING

In the warmer parts of the country your polytunnel or greenhouse may overheat despite good ventilation. It is quite easy to shade a greenhouse but it is a lot more difficult for a polytunnel. Traditionally a white wash with garden lime was used to paint the glass panes especially on the south and west side of the greenhouse. There are also commercial shading paints available that are much easier to apply. Only apply the paint in early summer and remove in late summer.

There are also various shading materials available that can be fixed on the outside of the greenhouse. The best are exterior blinds that can be rolled up in dull weather allowing for some flexibility.

Be aware though that shading your greenhouse in the less favourable parts of the country can be quite detrimental. In these areas every bit of heat is necessary for warmth loving crops, such as tomatoes, to ripen properly.

HEATING

This book only covers crops that can be grown in an unheated greenhouse or polytunnel. Heating the whole greenhouse or polytunnel is quite wasteful as the heat escapes quickly and nowadays there is really no point in heating the environment – we'd better keep the 'greenhouse effect' in the greenhouse.

With proper planning and timing you'll be able to grow nearly everything you want in your greenhouse or polytunnel whenever in season.

HYGIENE

Good hygiene in the greenhouse and polytunnel is essential for healthy plant growth. Pests and diseases can harbour in messy corners, on old plants and even on the plastic and glass.

Checklist

- Remove dead, diseased plants and plant parts as soon as you notice them.
- Remove debris (old pots, compost bags and anything else that's lying around).
- Clean the glass or plastic in late autumn once the summer crops are out. Scrub and wash the glass or plastic inside and outside using hot soapy water or a lemon based disinfectant (such as Citrox). You can use a long handled soft sweeping brush.
- If you have a heating bench with an electric cable in a sand base it's best to remove the sand once you don't need the propagator any longer (June) and set it up again in January.
- Clean and wash all modular trays and pots with hot water and washing up liquid.

PROPAGATION

PROPAGATION - SEED SOWING

A greenhouse or a polytunnel provides an excellent space for propagating your vegetable plants. If you have a heating bench you can start sowing from January onwards and thus extend your growing season.

Greenhouses – with their higher light transmission – are better for propagation, especially very early in the year where every ray of sunlight is so important to prevent your seedlings from getting too leggy.

Polytunnels are second best and you can simply delay sowing for a week or two.

Fig. 18. Propagation area in a tunnel

SUCCESSFUL GERMINATION

For successful germination you need viable seeds. They need to be fertilized and contain a living embryo. Seeds will deteriorate in storage. This affects the germination percentage, the germination time and also the vigour of the seedlings. On average, seeds store for 2–4 years in a cool, dry place. Parsnip and celery seeds, however, last only for one season. Seeds should never be left in a hot or damp polytunnel as they will deteriorate quickly!

CORRECT TEMPERATURE FOR GERMINATION

Each crop has got its minimum, optimum and maximum temperature for germination. Generally, the higher the temperature, the better the germination. On the other hand, too high a temperature can be detrimental (e.g. lettuce does not germinate well above 25°C). A good average temperature for most crops would be about 18–20°C.

There are different types of heated propagation units:
- Benches with electric cables on sand and thermostat.
- Heating pads with thermostat.
- Electrical propagators.
- Home-made unit using insulating material and electrical heat source, i.e. light bulbs.

Fig. 19. Heating bench.

TABLE 1: GERMINATION TEMPERATURE FOR VEGETABLE SEEDS

Crop	Germination temperature in °C			Days to germination under optimum temperature and moisture conditions
	Min	Opt	Max	
Beetroot	8	28	33	6
Broccoli	7	25	30	4
Brussels sprouts	6	30	33	4
Cabbage	10	30	35	4
Carrot	7	25	30	8
Cauliflower	8	23	30	5
Celery	15	20	24	7
Cucumber	20	30	35	3
Kale	10	32	37	4
Leek	8	25	30	7
Lettuce	7	18	23	3
Onion	10	23	33	7
Parsley	10	23	30	13
Parsnip	10	17	20	14
Pea	15	23	27	6
Pepper	18	30	37	8
Tomato	5	27	33	6
Turnip	15	30	38	3

MOISTURE AND AIR

Seeds need moisture and air to germinate. They need to imbibe 40–50 per cent water for germination to take place. The higher the temperature, the higher the water uptake will be. If there is too much water in the soil/compost the seeds may just rot away.

LIGHT

A few vegetable seeds require light to germinate, i.e. lettuce, celery. That means that you shouldn't cover these seeds with compost, just place them on the surface. Obviously, as soon as plants have germinated, they require light to photosynthesize. In winter and early spring, the natural light levels are quite low, so artificial light may be necessary to prevent plants from becoming leggy.

STORING SEEDS

Most vegetable seeds will keep easily for the next growing season provided they are kept cool and dry (exceptions are parsnips and celery). Never leave seed packets outside in the garden, in a polytunnel or in a damp shed or garage, because the high humidity will quickly ruin them. An air-tight glass jar or a ziplock bag is an ideal storage container. Seeds should be kept dry and stored at low temperatures. They should ideally be kept in your coolest room, or better still, in a fridge. Apart from parsnips and celery I use started seed packets for a second year and then buy new seeds. I'm aware that many seeds will keep for much longer but I find that the vigour of the plants decreases with age and thus the quality of vegetables will decrease as well.

SOWING METHODS

In theory all vegetables can be sown directly into the ground where they are to grow, and thinned out to their final spacing. However, raising plants indoors and transplanting them out has many advantages for a number of crops.

Direct sowing

When sowing directly into the soil ensure that the soil is loosened deep down and that the top surface of the soil is very fine and flat so that the tiny seeds won't fall down between the clods. Generally speaking, root crops such as carrots, beetroot, parsnips, swedes, turnips and radish don't transplant well and are therefore sown directly into the ground. Transplanting those crops may cause forking of their taproots (especially in carrots). Also vegetables with large seeds such as peas and beans are generally sown direct (to save space in the propagation house). Most other vegetables will perform much better if they are raised indoors and planted out at a later stage.

Transplanting

Many gardeners nowadays prefer to start their vegetable plants indoors in a glasshouse or south-facing windowsill. The process from sowing to planting may take about 4–10 weeks depending on the season and the crop. Most vegetables (excluding root crops) benefit from transplanting because: there is a more uniform plant stand in the plot; there is easier weed control as plants are weeks ahead of the weeds; it shortens the growing period in the garden so allowing more crops to be grown on the same land than could be achieved by sowing directly into the soil; and transplanting is also used for plants whose seeds are too difficult to germinate in the garden (e.g. celery, which has tiny seeds); also there is less wastage of seeds as no thinning is required. This is very important where seeds are very expensive (e.g. hybrid seeds).

The main disadvantage of transplanting is that the plant roots can get damaged during planting. The plants could suffer because the leaves lose water through transpiration and it can't be fully replenished by the roots. The plants suffer until new roots are produced. This transplanting shock is a big problem with bare root transplants but not at all with modular transplants.

Modular or cell trays

Modular trays are becoming the most popular method of transplant raising. There are now many different types of plastic trays available with different numbers and sizes of modules (also called cells or plugs). There are some good quality trays on sale which will last you for many years but also some very cheap and quite useless ones.

Advantages
- Good crop establishment.
- Uniform plant development.
- Faster transplanting, thus
- Reducing labour requirement.

Disadvantages
- Relatively high cost of trays.
- A high degree of management skills required to produce quality transplants in cells with a very limited volume of compost, reserve of nutrients and water-holding capacity.

SOWING DEPTH

Seeds need a good contact with the soil so they need to be sown in drills and covered with soil. However, if the seeds are sown too deeply they may not have enough reserves to be able to reach the surface of the soil. On the other hand if seeds are sown too shallow, the germinating seeds are more likely to dry out. Small seeds only have small reserves and should be sown shallow.

SUCCESSFUL TRANSPLANTING

Here are a few tips to get better establishment of the transplants:

Hardening off

Hardening off will not be necessary if you plant out into the polytunnel or greenhouse. However, transplants can still experience shock when they are suddenly taken off a warm heating bench. If at all possible you could start to lower the temperature of the bench a few days before and remove the plants in the morning. This is not always possible as there are always plants at different stages on the bench. I usually leave the more warmth loving vegetables, such as tomatoes, peppers, cucumbers, courgette and basil, on the heating bench until May when the weather is more favourable.

Transplant when plants are ready
Don't let your transplants get pot-bound in the modules. Modular transplants should be planted as soon as the root ball comes out easily without the compost falling off it. The longer you leave them after that, the more stressed they get.

Transplant in dull weather and in the evening
The best time of day to plant out is during dull weather in the evening. If you plant out your seedlings in the morning on a beautiful hot sunny day they are likely to wilt due to extensive evaporation. This applies only during the warmer periods.

SEED COMPOSTS
Germination will take place without any nutrients – indeed better than with nutrients. However, seedlings require a balance of the main nutrients (N, P, K/nitrogen, phosphorus, potassium) as well as trace elements to sustain plant growth for a short period. High levels of nitrogen will inhibit germination and may even damage the roots of seedlings. As the plants develop they require more nutrients for their growth. When the seedlings are potted on, a richer compost should be chosen or alternatively liquid feeding will be necessary to sustain healthy plant growth.

Sources of organic compost

There are now various suppliers of excellent organic seed and potting composts. There are even some organic peat-free composts. Do ensure though that these are certified organic composts. Unfortunately it is still legal to call a non-organic compost 'organic' even if it is not certified. This also applies to fertilizers such as poultry pellets, so if you are in doubt please ask the supplier who the organic certification body is and the relevant certification number. If there isn't one, it's not really organic and I think it's terrible to cheat people and make them believe it's organic.

Table 2 (overleaf) shows an overview of my preferred sowing method for each vegetable. This is especially for tunnel or greenhouse production where growing space is more valuable. This is based on my own experience, so other gardeners may prefer different methods. You will soon find out what works best for you!

TABLE 2: SOWING METHOD FOR EACH VEGETABLE

Vegetable	Preferred sowing method	Number of seeds per cell	Sowing depth (in cm)	Time from sowing to planting (in weeks)
Aubergine	Transplant	5 seeds per 7cm pot, prick out into 9cm pot	1.5	12–14
Basil	Transplant	4	1.5	4–5
Bean, French	Sow in 9cm pots	4	3–4	5
Bean, Runner	Sow in 9cm pots	4	3–4	5
Beetroot	Direct sown		1.5	
Cabbage, Chinese	Transplant	1	2.2	4–5
Cabbages, all	Transplant	1	2.2	4–5
Calabrese	Transplant	1	2.2	4–5
Carrots	Direct		1.5	
Cauliflower	Transplant	1	2.2	4–5
Celery	Sow in open seed tray, then prick out into modular tray	1 seedling per cell	1	8–10

Vegetable	Preferred sowing method	Number of seeds per cell	Sowing depth (in cm)	Time from sowing to planting (in weeks)
Chervil	Transplant	5	1.5	3–4
Claytonia	Transplant	5–7	1	5
Coriander	Transplant	5–7	2	3–4
Courgette	Sow in 7cm pots	1	2	4
Cucumber	Sow in 7cm pots	1	2	6–8
Dill	Transplant	5	1.5	3–4
Endive	Transplant	1	1	5
Fennel, Florence	Transplant	1	1.5	5
Garlic	Direct planted			
Kohlrabi	Transplant	1	2.2	4–5
Leeks	Transplant	2	1.5	7–8
Lettuce	Transplant	1 (or 4 for leaf production)	1 (surface)	3–4
Melon	Sow in 7cm pots	1	2	6–8
Oca	Direct planted			
Onion (sets)	Direct planted			
Onion (seeds)	Transplant	4	1.5	7–8
Oriental Salads	Transplant	5	1.5	3–4

227

Vegetable	Preferred sowing method	Number of seeds per cell	Sowing depth (in cm)	Time from sowing to planting (in weeks)
Pea	Direct sown		3.5	
Pepper	Sow in 9cm pots	5–7 Prick out	1	15
Physalis	Sow in 9cm pots	5–7 Prick out	1	12–14
Radish	Direct sown		2.2	
Rocket, Salad	Transplant (or direct)	5	1.5	3–4
Scallions (Spring onion)	Transplant	10	1.5	4–6
Spinach, Annual	Transplant (or direct)	4	1.5	4
Spinach, Perpetual	Transplant (or direct)	1 (thin to one)	2	4–5
Squash	Transplant	1 seed per 7cm pot	2.5	5
Sweetcorn	Transplant	1 seed per 7cm pot	3.5	4–5
Swiss Chard	Transplant (or direct)	1 (thin to one)	2	4–5
Tomato	Sow in 9cm pots	5–7 Prick out		

SOIL FERTILITY

There is a very simple rule: the healthier your soil is, the healthier your crops will be.

With gardening, everything starts with the soil. If you manage to create a fertile, healthy and living soil you are already half way there to growing delicious and healthy food for your family. A well-structured soil allows plant roots to penetrate easily and find available nutrients and water. We have to learn how to care for our soil and improve it. But first of all we have to understand that any crop or weed that we remove from our soil contains nutrients that have been taken up by these plants.

Obviously a cabbage is greedier than a lettuce. These nutrients have to be returned on a regular basis otherwise we exploit our soil and make it infertile. In a polytunnel or greenhouse we produce a lot more food compared to an outdoor plot. We sometimes get four or five different vegetables into the same space in one year. That simply means we need to feed it a lot more.

We might not all be blessed to inherit a fertile soil but what greater satisfaction could there be than to make your soil fertile for your own benefit and for future generations? The good news is that every soil can be made fertile and the magic ingredient to achieve this is compost or composted manure.

Good compost and manure can revitalize a lifeless soil. It improves the structure, imbibes the soil with life and provides all the necessary plant foods. I strongly believe that such a soil will grow vegetables that will feed us properly; it will grow healthy vegetables and hopefully keep us healthy too.

There is a stunning fact: **In one handful of fertile soil there are more living creatures than there are people on the earth!**

All those soil organisms play a significant role in maintaining a healthy fertile soil. If these organisms were not present the soil would have no life – it would die. Their role is to break down the crop residues and other natural inputs and mix them with the soil. As they break down the waste, essential plant nutrients are being made available to plants. They are single-handedly responsible for the renewal of life.

And there is another great invention of nature: the warmer the soil, the more active these micro-organisms are and the more nutrients they release. That's also when plants need more nutrients.

So how do we encourage these creatures? We simply feed them with compost, manure, crop residues, seaweed, weeds, etc.

To summarize

A healthy soil produces healthy vegetables, so if your plants are ailing the first question you should ask yourself: is my soil fertile enough?

IMPROVING YOUR SOIL

Your polytunnel and greenhouse soil will have to be made a lot more fertile than your outdoor plot. A tomato plant that produces over two hundred tomatoes will require a much more fertile soil than a crop of beetroot or carrots outdoors.

Any type of soil can be improved with compost or other organic matter applications. A sticky clay soil will become looser and more friable and thus the drainage will be improved. A sandy soil that easily loses water and nutrients will be able to hold onto the nutrients and moisture.

In order to improve a poor greenhouse or tunnel soil I would apply one wheelbarrow of compost or composted manure to every three square metres of soil once a year. This should be incorporated into the soil with a fork or spade well in advance of sowing or planting. Once your fertility levels are up, a much smaller annual application of organic matter is sufficient.

SOURCES OF ORGANIC MATTER
(FOR FEEDING AND FOR SOIL IMPROVEMENT)

Well-rotted strawy manure

Ensure that the manure is really well broken down. It should smell quite pleasant and be fairly crumbly. It will supply plant nutrients as well as improve the structure of the soil. Hungry crops such as cucumbers and tomatoes will benefit from manure applications. It is best to incorporate the manure a couple of weeks before planting.

Well-decomposed garden compost

Unfortunately we can never produce enough of our own black gold. Well-decomposed compost is similar to well-rotted manure except that the nutrients are more slowly available. There is less of a danger of overfeeding when you use compost. I prefer to use compost for the less greedy crops. The application rate can be higher.

Well-decomposed leaf mould compost

If you pile up autumn leaves and leave them for a couple of years you will get a wonderful leaf mould compost that is very much like forest soil. Leaf mould will improve the structure of soils but will not supply nutrients so any amount can be applied. If it hasn't fully decomposed though there is a danger that it will rob the nitrogen from your soil (nitrogen immobilization).

Worm cast compost

If you can get hold of a cheap source of worm cast compost you'll be lucky. It's the best soil improver of all. Unfortunately it is also quite expensive. You could consider having your own wormery. Half a bucket per square metre is ideal.

Garden centre products

Most garden centres stock bagged composted manure, composts and soil conditioners. These are ideal for people with city gardens or no access to other sources. Follow the directions on the bag.

Municipal or greenwaste compost

Throughout the country there are an increasing number of compost manufacturers. Some of them produce excellent composts. It is well worth finding out where your nearest manufacturer is. The application rate is one bucket per square metre.

FEEDING ESTABLISHED PLANTS

The mantra of organic gardening is: 'Feed your soil and not your plants' and not the other way round. The idea is that a fertile soil will provide adequate nutrition for your vegetables.

Unfortunately it isn't always perfect and our plants require more food than the soil can provide. This sometimes happens in late summer when the tomatoes and cucumbers are at their most prolific and 'greediest'. In these occasions there is a need for an additional feed such as:

Liquid feeds

Liquid feeds can be made quite simply by putting certain plants, comfrey or compost into a barrel of water. They can give struggling plants a quick boost as they provide plant nutrients in a quickly available form.

I usually mix a few ingredients together. For a 200 litre water barrel I use a bucket of good compost, two buckets of seaweed and two buckets of chopped nettles. I place the ingredients into one or two large potato sacks and suspend them in the filled water barrel. I also add quantities of comfrey leaves whenever they are ready to cut. There is no need to put the comfrey leaves into the bags as they dissolve in the water.

I start using the mixture about a month after making it at a dilution of 1 part liquid feed to 10 parts water. The barrel can be topped up with water and more comfrey leaves.

Top-dressing with organic poultry pellets

Organic poultry pellets can provide a quick-fix solution to starving plants. The nutrients from the pellets become available to plants very quickly. There is a product available that composts poultry manure with seaweed prior to making it into pellets giving excellent results. But don't rely on it completely – only view it as a supplementary feed. Never give up on your compost or manure.

PEST AND DISEASE CONTROL

Pests and diseases will often thrive in the damp, warm environment of a polytunnel or greenhouse. In this environment they can multiply very quickly and reduce the yield of your plants or even kill them.

PESTS

Pests cause damage to your plants by eating them. Anything that is bigger than a micro-organism is classed as a pest.

Common greenhouse pests include the greenhouse whitefly, leatherjackets, red spider mite, etc.

DISEASES

Diseases are caused by micro-organisms such as bacteria, viruses and fungi. Bacterial damage is manifested in lesions. They are not as easy to identify. Virus diseases affect the vigour of the plant. They rarely kill a plant but they always reduce the yield and distort plants. Symptoms include yellow mottling, concentric ring-spots or yellow mosaic areas.

Virus diseases are easily transmitted by sap-sucking insects such as aphids as well as with pruning knives and secateurs.

Fungi can easily be recognized by their fruiting bodies, such as the grey mould of botrytis or the white growth of powdery mildew.

DISORDERS

Physiological disorders are not caused by pests or diseases. They are the result of environmental factors. Yellowing of the leaves can be caused by over-watering or through a deficiency in the soil.

Common plant disorders include blossom end rot, fruit splitting and tipburn.

PREVENTION IS BETTER THAN CURE

The aim of organic gardening is to provide a healthy garden by creating a fertile living soil, increasing biodiversity in your garden and implementing a suitable crop rotation. All emphasis should be placed on preventing pests and diseases rather than having to react to them. In fact, once a pest or disease establishes itself on your crops there is often very little you can do to control it effectively.

Protecting your plants from pests and diseases begins long before the crops are sown or planted in your garden. Whilst it is impossible and even counter-productive to completely eliminate pests and diseases, a combination of the following tips will definitely lessen problems in your tunnel or greenhouse.

Soil fertility

A healthy soil produces healthy plants. The care of your soil is the most important duty of every gardener. It is the most effective method of preventing a pest or disease outbreak. The ideal soil is a loose, moist humus-rich soil full of worms and other soil life with a balanced nutrient content, including all the trace elements. It may take a good few years to achieve this, but even the poorest soil can be made very fertile using organic methods.

Crop rotation

Vegetables that belong to the same family should be grouped together and not be grown in the same bed in the tunnel or greenhouse for a number of years. Obviously it is much more difficult to plan a rotation in a tunnel or greenhouse as there are often a number of crops in each bed in one particular year and the space is often too small to allow for a sufficient break. We can only try our best.

Ventilation

Good ventilation is an absolute necessity for minimizing plant diseases as they thrive in humid conditions and can spread at an alarming rate. Ventilation can also prevent extreme temperature fluctuations between day and night time.

Correct watering

Both dry and wet soil conditions will weaken your plants and make them more susceptible to pests and diseases. Ensure that you have a proper watering regime.

Biodiversity

A garden with good biodiversity is a lot less prone to sudden attacks of pests and diseases as there is a balance of pests and predators. This is not easily achieved in a tunnel or greenhouse. You could, however, plant a few insect attracting flowers such as the Poached Egg Plant at both entrances to lure in beneficial insects.

You can also have a miniature pond in the corner and bring in a few tadpoles.

Hygiene

Hygiene in your tunnel or greenhouse is very important for pest and disease control. This includes weed control and removal of damaged or diseased leaves or plants from the garden.

Good seeds

You should always start with good and clean seeds. They should be stored in a cool, dry place and not for too many years. I usually keep seeds only for a second year and then buy new ones. New seeds are a lot more vigorous.

Healthy transplants

Only plant the best transplants. A poor transplant often makes a poor vegetable and will be the first that gets infected by pests and diseases. It is very rare that all transplants in a tray are of the same quality. You should always sow a few more modules than you need to compensate.

Right plant, right place

Plants that are not suited to your climate and soil conditions will never thrive and therefore will be the first ones to be attacked by pests and diseases. In a tunnel or greenhouse make sure that sun- and heat-loving plants such as peppers, chillies, aubergines and basil are not in the shade of taller plants such as tomatoes or cucumbers. On the other hand, crops like celery, dill, coriander and lettuce will do better in summer if planted in semi-shade.

Resistant varieties

Plant breeders have done amazing work in developing new varieties which are resistant (completely or to a certain extent) to plant diseases and even pests. The Hungarian Sarpo potatoes are one of the best examples but there are many other vegetables. If you find that you have a recurring problem with certain crops look out for a resistant variety and that might cure the problem. Here are some examples:

- Potato: Sarpo Axona, Sarpo Mira, Orla and Setanta are very resistant to blight.
- Pea: Hurst Greenshaft is very resistant to mildew.
- Lettuce: Sylvesta is resistant to leaf aphids.
- Lettuce: Matador is resistant to downy mildew.
- Tomato: Ferline is resistant to blight.
- Tomato: Shirley F1 is resistant to greenback.

There are many more examples and you will find them when you browse through seed catalogues.

Timing of sowing

The advantage of growing vegetables in a tunnel or greenhouse is that you grow them out of season when most pests and diseases are not yet around. If you sow your early carrots in late January they will be harvested before the rootfly is ready to attack. The same applies for first early potatoes – they will never get blight.

Breaking the cycle

You could have brassicas (cabbage family) growing in your tunnel or greenhouse all year round. This makes it very easy for all pests and diseases to survive and re-infect new crops. I never grow any member of the cabbage family indoors from May until September.

Adjusting the spacing

If plants are spaced too closely they are a lot more susceptible to fungal diseases such as grey mould or mildew. If you want to lessen any potential problem you can always space your crops a little bit further apart. This increases the airflow through the crop and reduces the incidence of fungal diseases that thrive in more humid conditions.

Proper sowing and planting

Good care should be taken when sowing seeds and planting vegetables. The better they start off the more likely they will do well.

MANAGING PESTS AND DISEASES

Whilst many pest and disease problems can be prevented, there are various occasions where pest or disease numbers increase to such high numbers that they can cause serious damage to your crops.

It is crucial to properly identify the culprits. It often happens that an innocent bystander found at the scene is accused of the act when it may in fact have been the one who has just eaten the offender.

Mechanical control
Netting

Mechanical controls include barriers that keep pests away from your crops. There are various types of netting available to protect your vegetables (fleece, crop covers, Bionet, bird netting).

Collars
Collars are used around brassicas to prevent the cabbage root fly from laying its eggs near the cabbage stems.

Traps
Many pests can be lured into traps. The beer trap for slugs is a popular example. If you use this, ensure that the lip of the container is above the soil surface or you may also catch some ground beetles which would have eaten many more slugs than you have caught. Personally I can think of a much better use of beer!

Handpicking
Handpicking larger pests such as slugs, leatherjackets or caterpillars can be quite efficient especially in a small garden. I know some gardeners who get great satisfaction out of it.

Biological control
Biological control includes attracting beneficial creatures that feed on pests as well as introducing predators for the job! These predators can be purchased by mail order and are usually very effective in a tunnel or greenhouse especially if used at the right time when the pests start to appear.

Examples of natural predators include
- Hoverflies – the larvae and adult hoverfly feed on aphids.
- Lacewing – feed on aphids.
- Ladybirds – feed on aphids.
- Beetles – feed on slugs and many other small pests.
- Earwigs – most people consider them pests but they feed on aphids.
- Frogs – feed on slugs.

Examples of introduced biological control

- Predatory mite (*Phytoseiulus persimilis*) controls glasshouse red spider mite
- Parasitic wasps (*Encarsia formosa*) control glasshouse whitefly
- Predatory midge larva (*Aphidoletes aphidimyza*) controls aphids
- Parasitic wasps (*Aphidius* sp.) controls aphids
- Nematodes (*Heterorhabditis* sp.) controls vine weevil grubs
- Bacterium (*Bacillus thuringiensis*) controls caterpillars on brassicas
- Parasitic nematode (*Phasmarhabditis* sp.) controls slugs

Chemical control

There are a number of so called 'safe' organic sprays available to the gardener. They are safe in the way that they are fully biodegradable within a couple of days (with the exception of copper sulphate) but nearly all of them will also kill beneficial insects and thus disrupt the natural cycles so I won't mention them in this book.

The garlic spray is one exception. It masks the smell of host plants so that pests find it less attractive or even get confused. It also strengthens the plants so that they become more resistant to pest and disease attacks.

Garlic contains sulphur which is a natural antibacterial and antifungal agent. Press six cloves of garlic and soak for 24 hours in a tablespoon of vegetable oil. Strain the mixture and add one litre of water. The mixture can be stored and used as required. The dilution rate is 1:10 (garlic mix/water) and is best applied with a spray bottle.

A milk/water spray (1 part milk and 7 parts water) was probably the best new discovery in organic disease control. I have successfully used it to control diseases such as grey mould and mildew on a variety of vegetables. You can spray it with a little plant spray directly onto affected plant parts ideally 3 days in a row and the disease stops spreading further. Unfortunately it didn't work for potato blight.

The most interesting spray is a **compost tea** or extract. You soak one part of compost with 10 parts of water for about a week and stir it daily. You then dilute it with another 10 parts of water before spraying it onto susceptible crops to prevent fungal diseases. Many scientists all over the world achieve tremendous results in controlling a large variety of diseases.

COMMON GREENHOUSE PESTS
Aphids

Aphids are one of the most common and serious pests in your tunnel or greenhouse. They thrive in the shelter and warmth of your indoor space. There are many different species, often adapted to just one or two host plants. They feed by sucking the sap out of plants and thus weakening them and making them more susceptible to fungal diseases. They also transmit virus diseases from one plant to another. They have an amazing reproductive rate so that their colonies can double within a day.

Prevention and control

- Attract natural predators (ladybirds, lacewings, hoverflies) with certain plants (Tagetes, Poached Egg Plant, Phacelia).
- Avoid over-fertilizing as aphids prefer soft, lush growth.
- Purchase predators (*Aphidoletes* and *Aphidius* sp.) by mail order.
- Hose them off with a spray of water.
- You can also buy yellow sticky tape from garden centres to catch flying pests such as aphids. They are very good as indicators to find out which pests you have but they will not control pests sufficiently.

Root aphids

Root aphids live on young roots near the soil surface. The lettuce root aphid is probably the most common as well as serious pest.

The symptoms are drooping and dull looking plants. If you pull them you'll notice white wool-like growth around the roots and when you look closely you can see the small white aphids.

Prevention and control

• Adopt a sound crop rotation.
• Avoid planting lettuce into affected borders for two years.
• Don't leave your plants in the ground for too long.

Slugs and snails

Slugs and snails are one of the most hated creatures in the garden. They can also be quite a nuisance in your tunnel or greenhouse especially if it's a bit untidy. They hide during the day and come out to feed at night. On very dull and wet days they even feed during the day.

Prevention and control

• A tidy tunnel or greenhouse won't quite eliminate slugs but it will definitely reduce their number substantially.
• Create a small pond in the corner of the tunnel to attract frogs.
• Use organic slug pellets (Ferramol).
• Use biological control (Nemaslug).
• Trap them with small pieces of timber or slates and collect them every morning. After a few days you'll find that you have also attracted ground beetles under the wood and they in turn will feed on the slugs and slug eggs.
• Do not use beer traps if you catch beetles that would naturally feed on slugs. If you do use beer traps ensure that they are not level with the soil to prevent beetles from falling in.

Glasshouse whitefly (*Trialeurodes vaporariorum*)

These are tiny white moth-like aphids that usually affect your tomatoes, peppers and aubergines. They live on the undersides of leaves and fly off when disturbed. They feed on the plant sap and secrete a sticky honeydew on which sooty moulds will grow soon after. The whitefly usually overwinters on plants and weeds in the tunnel or greenhouse and in the following year will multiply rapidly. The glasshouse whitefly is not a native species and was introduced into Europe with some tomato plants from Mexico. It can only survive indoors. So if you have a new tunnel or greenhouse you can very easily avoid this most annoying pest by raising all your tomato, pepper and aubergine plants from seed, because the only way of introducing it is through plants.

Prevention and control
- Do not buy in susceptible plants.
- Clear and tidy your tunnel and greenhouse in the autumn to eliminate overwintering places.
- Hose off with a jet of water.
- Use the garlic spray on a weekly basis before the whitefly appears.
- Use yellow sticky traps to show you when they start.
- Introduce the biological control *Encarsia formosa* as soon as you notice the first whitefly

Leatherjackets
Leatherjackets are the larvae of the crane fly ('daddy long legs'). They feed on the roots and stems of many different plants causing considerable losses of young plants, especially lettuce. In the tunnel or greenhouse, leatherjackets are most active in early spring usually coinciding with your first lettuce plantings in March and April and that's the time you have to be alert.

Prevention and control
- You should check your young lettuce plants daily and as soon as you notice that the plants look wilted pull the wilted plants out and check if the stem has been nibbled. Carefully search the soil where the plant was growing and often you will find the culprit.

- You can also try to trap them by placing a layer of lawn mowings on the ground and cover this with thick cardboard or black plastic. After 2 days you can check the trap and dispose of any larvae.

Red spider mite (*Tetranychus urticae*)

Red spider mites often affect cucumbers and French beans and sometimes also aubergines and strawberries. The first symptoms are a light mottling of the leaves. Tiny green mites are visible with a magnifying glass on the underside of the leaves. Only the over-wintering female mites have a bright red colour.

When the mite numbers increase, the leaves become more and more discoloured and covered in a fine white web. The older leaves turn yellow and brittle. The red spider mites prefer hot and dry conditions.

Prevention and control

During dry conditions increase the humidity by spraying the leaves of your cucumber plants regularly. Anyway they prefer a humid atmosphere. Clean out the tunnel and greenhouse thoroughly in autumn to eliminate potential hibernation places. If you find that you get them every year, be prepared and introduce a biological control as soon as the problem starts. The biological control is a slightly larger mite called *Phytoseiulus persimilis* and it feeds on the red spider mite but does no damage to your cucumbers.

Tomato moth *(Lacanobia oleracea)*

The caterpillars of this moth eat holes in the leaves and fruit of your tomato plants. They are usually green with a yellow stripe along their body. The green is very much the colour of the tomato leaves so they are hard to spot. The damage is quite obvious though.

Prevention and control

Clean out the tunnel or greenhouse thoroughly in late autumn. During the growing season inspect your tomato plants regularly and remove any caterpillars that are nibbling away on your tomato leaves.

Cutworms

Cutworms are the caterpillars of various moth species. They are usually grey or brown, quite fat and up to 4cm long. They live just under the soil surface and feed on root vegetables, brassicas and lettuce. As with leatherjackets they often sever the stem at ground level and they can also be found near affected plants.

Prevention and control

As with the leatherjackets, check newly planted lettuce and brassica plants and try to find the grubs before they do more damage.

Millipedes

Millipedes have two pairs of legs per segment whereas the beneficial centipedes have only one pair per segment. There are many different types of millipedes and they may sometimes damage seedlings. I have never experienced them as being a major problem so I leave them in peace.

Vine weevil

Vine weevils are small, brown wingless weevils which hide by day and feed on leaves during the night. The larvae of the vine weevil cause most damage as they usually appear in vast numbers and feed on plant roots. Many pot plants such as begonias, primulas and cyclamen are their favourite, but they also feed on strawberries. The only way to get them is by you yourself introducing them with a fated flower pot from a different garden.

Prevention and control

- Be careful what plants you buy in and, if necessary, check the roots. Any time you pot on a plant look out for signs of root damage. If a pot plant wilts suddenly check immediately for the larvae and get rid of them.

- There is also a biological control – parasitic nematodes – that can be watered on to pots and the soil. They are only effective if it is warm enough so only apply from May onwards.

Wireworms
Wireworms are the larvae of the click beetle. They are thin, orange-brown larvae about 2cm long with a hard body and three pairs of legs near the head. They kill seedlings by feeding on young stems and roots. They can also tunnel through potatoes and carrots. I'm not aware of any organic control method apart from hand picking them whenever you come across one when digging.

COMMON DISEASES

A tunnel or greenhouse environment provides ideal conditions for many plant diseases. Good soil conditions, ventilation and appropriate watering can reduce the problems.

Grey mould *(Botrytis cinerea)*
This is one of the most common plant diseases which affects a wide range of plants, especially cucumbers, tomatoes, beans, lettuce and strawberries. The symptoms are white-grey fungal growth on affected areas. The disease spreads by spores that are released in clouds when touched. The problem is worse in cool, damp and overcrowded conditions.
Prevention and control
- It is difficult to control so keep your garden clean and remove any diseased leaves as soon as you notice them.
- Avoid overcrowding plants so that there is good air-circulation between the plants.
- Good ventilation is essential.
- Never water in the evening.
- Spray with milk/water mix onto the affected parts.

Powdery mildew

Powdery mildew is a disease that is caused by various fungi. The symptoms are a powdery white coating on the leaves. Most gardeners will have seen it on courgettes. It can also affect cucumbers, strawberries and grapes but they do not spread from one type to another as there are different fungi responsible for each host plant. The problem is worse in hot, dry and overcrowded conditions. The spores overwinter in crop residues.

Prevention and control
- Avoid overcrowding plants so that there is good air-circulation between the plants.
- Remove the lower leaves of plants for better air-circulation.
- Keep plants well watered.
- Spray with milk/water mix onto the affected parts.

Downy mildew

Downy mildew is not as obvious and easily recognized as powdery mildew. It is a more off-white mould and usually occurs in cool damp conditions. The fungal agents are *Bremia* and *Peronospora*. In the tunnel and greenhouse, winter and early spring lettuce is the most affected plant. The symptoms are pale patches on the leaves with corresponding patches of mould on the underside of the leaves.

Prevention and control
- Crop rotation.
- Avoid overcrowding.
- Use resistant varieties of lettuce (there are plenty of them available).
- Do not water in the evening.
- Remove and dispose of infected plant material (not in the compost).

Damping off

Damping off can be caused by various fungi and bacteria. It's a devastating disease as whole batches of seedlings can topple over and die, more or less from one day to another. The problem is worse in cool, damp and overcrowded conditions.

Prevention and control
- Clean and sterilize pots and trays.
- Use a good seed compost that has good drainage.
- Sow thinly.
- Don't overwater.

Potato blight *(Phytophthora infestans)*

Every gardener knows about potato blight. The spores of this disease sometimes blow into your tunnel or greenhouse and then wipe out your tomato crop. Tomatoes and potatoes are closely related and both belong to the Nightshade family. The disease spreads fastest in warm humid conditions. The symptoms are dark blotches on the leaves with a white mould on the underside of the leaves. The symptom on the tomato fruit is a dry brown rot.

Prevention and control
Blight is such a powerful fungus there is very little you can do to stop it. The best prevention is to use a resistant tomato variety such as Ferline and there may be more varieties available.

Root and foot rots

Root and foot rots are caused by a variety of fungi. The symptoms include wilted leaves and blackened roots. Cucumbers are very susceptible to this disease but tomatoes, lettuce and strawberries may also suffer from it. It is a fatal disease and there is no cure for it. The plants just keel over and die. This is such a nuisance especially for cucumbers that are very precious plants.

Prevention and control
- Rotate susceptible crops.

- Do not plant your cucumbers deeper than they were in the pots. I used to make this mistake, mainly because of all the aerial roots at the base of the stem.

Cucumber mosaic virus

This virus disease affects all members of the cucumber family (Cucurbits). The symptoms are mosaic patterns on the leaves and sometimes even distorted fruits. The disease is passed on to other plants by aphids and is also carried by the common weed 'chickweed'.

Prevention and control

There is no cure for this disease. The only way of overcoming it is to grow a resistant variety the following year.

Tobacco mosaic virus

This virus affects all members of the Nightshade family – potatoes, tomatoes, aubergines, peppers, nicotiana and tobacco. It is a very infectious disease and smokers can transmit it to tomatoes when they side-shoot the plants.

The symptoms include mottling and wilting of the leaves.

Prevention and control

Again there is no cure for this disease and the only way of overcoming it is to grow a resistant variety the following year.

COMMON DISORDERS

Blossom end rot

It is quite a common disorder of tomatoes. The symptoms are a hard, dark brown area at the blossom end of the fruit. It is usually caused be lack of calcium uptake when the soil or compost is too dry.

Prevention and control

Check the pH level of your soil and apply ground limestone or calcified seaweed if it is too acidic. Also water regularly to facilitate calcium uptake to the plant.

Splitting

Various vegetables are susceptible to splitting. These include radishes, tomatoes, potatoes and carrots. The cause is usually rapid growth after watering following a period where there was little growth during dry periods (or a lack of watering).

Prevention and control

- Water regularly.
- Apply compost to increase the water-holding capacity.
- Choose a resistant variety. The tomato 'Shirley F1' is much less prone to splitting compared to 'Gardener's Delight'.

Tip burn

Tip burn affects lettuce especially if grown in a tunnel or greenhouse. It is such a nuisance as the whole crop can be destroyed. The symptoms are scorched edges especially around the heart of the lettuce. It is caused when more water evaporates from the leaves than the plant can take up. This is often the case in a hot tunnel or greenhouse. It is also linked to a lack of calcium.

Prevention and control

- Water regularly.
- Mist the greenhouse or tunnel in the late morning during hot days.
- Ventilate.
- Check the pH level of your soil and apply ground limestone or calcified seaweed if it is too acidic.

NUTRIENT DISORDERS

Too much or too little of a particular plant nutrient can cause problems for your vegetables. It's important to be able to identify what's wrong with your plants and what you can do to make them better. Luckily, when you apply sufficient compost, most of your plants' needs should be covered.

Nitrogen deficiency
The symptoms are poor growth and pale leaves, sometimes with purple tints.

Nitrogen surplus
Lush growth, large leaves, very few flowers and fruit.

Magnesium deficiency
Yellowing between leaf veins especially on the older leaves.

Iron deficiency
Yellowing between the veins especially on the younger leaves. Often caused by a high pH when iron becomes unavailable.

ROTATION

Crop rotations can be very easily implemented in your outdoor vegetable garden. Indoors it becomes a lot more complex because there is limited space and you are likely to grow a number of different crops in each bed every year.

WHAT IS A CROP ROTATION?
The principle of crop rotation is to group related vegetables together and move them around your tunnel or greenhouse so that they do not grow on the same plot for a number of years.

BENEFITS OF ROTATION
Pest and disease control
Pest and disease pathogens can build up to catastrophic levels if the same host crops are grown in the same place year after year. If you move your crops around you interrupt the cycles of those pests and diseases. A crop rotation is only effective for soil-borne pests and diseases that are specific to a particular plant family.

However, crop rotation is essential in limiting the spread of the following soil-borne pests and diseases:
• Clubroot on brassicas (cabbage family)
• Nematodes on potatoes
• White rot on alliums (onion family).

Soil fertility
Vegetables differ in what they take out of the soil and what they give back to it. If you include peas and beans in your rotation they will add nitrogen to the soil. A leguminous green manure in your rotation will add even more.

On the other hand if you grow only heavy feeders such as cabbages your soil may quickly get tired.

Soil structure

A well-designed rotation can help in improving the structure of your soil. Some crops have a very deep taproot which can penetrate into the subsoil and extract nutrients from low down. Thus you should alternate deep-rooting vegetables (or green manures) with shallow-rooting ones.

Weed control

If you alternate weed-susceptible crops such as onions with weed-suppressing crops such as potatoes or cabbages, the weed problems for the susceptible crops may be lessened.

HOW LONG SHOULD THE ROTATION BE?

A three- or four-year rotation is ideal for a tunnel or greenhouse.

Step by step guide to planning your rotation

1. Make a list of all the vegetables you want to grow.
2. Group the vegetables into plant families.
3. Divide up the tunnel or greenhouse into equal plots.
4. Decide which families will be grouped together.
5. Draw up a plan.

Figs 20 and 21 show a sample rotation for a small tunnel or greenhouse with three beds. The central bed is wider as it can be reached from both sides.

The tall crops such as tomatoes, cucumbers, climbing French beans and sweetcorn can only be grown in the centre bed due to the height of the structure. These crops follow a separate three-year rotation.

All other vegetables are grown on the outside beds and follow a separate four-year rotation as can be seen in the illustrations.

VEGETABLE FAMILIES

Brassicaceae (Cabbage family)
Brussels sprouts
Broccoli
Cabbage
Calabrese
Cauliflower
Kale
Kohlrabi
Oriental brassicas (mustard, cress,
   mizuna, etc.)
Pak choi
Rocket
Radish
Swede
Turnip

Leguminosae (Pea family)
Pea
Bean

Solanaceae (Potato family)
Aubergine
Pepino
Pepper
Potato
Tomato

Umbelliferae (Carrot family)
Carrot
Celeriac
Celery
Florence fennel
Parsnips
Annual herbs: dill, coriander,
   chervil, parsley

Compositae (Daisy family)
Chicory
Endive
Globe artichoke
Jerusalem artichoke
Lettuce
Salsify
Scorzonera

Alliaceae (Onion family)
Garlic
Leek
Onion
Scallion
Shallot

Chenopodiaceae (Beetroot family)
Beetroot
Chard
Spinach

Cucurbitaceae (Cucumber family)
Courgette
Cucumber
Marrow
Melon
Pumpkin
Squash

Unrelated vegetables
Corn salad
Lemon verbena
Oca
Stevia
Sweetcorn
Winter purslane
Yacon

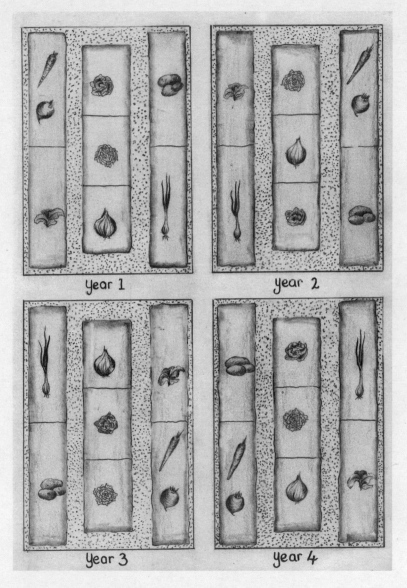

Fig. 20. Winter and Spring Rotation Plan.

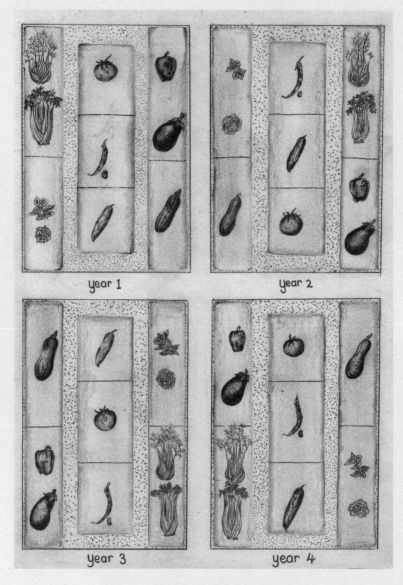

year 1

year 2

year 3

year 4

Fig. 21. Summer and Autumn Rotation Plan.

MONTH BY MONTH GUIDE

JANUARY

January can be the beginning of your creative gardening year in your greenhouse or polytunnel. You can start off new seedlings on your propagator and sow and plant the first vegetables into the ground. I always think that the first sowings and plantings are the most special and you are not yet in a rush and can still relax and enjoy the work.

Buy yourself a garden diary and take note of when and what you sow, which varieties perform well, what crops do well and which ones can be improved. A garden diary is as good as any university – it helps you to learn from your own experience and nothing can surpass your own local knowledge that is specific to your own soil and site.

You should also order your seeds, seed potatoes, onion sets and garlic bulbs now if you haven't done so yet. It's always handy to have them ready when you need them.

It's also time to plan your indoor cropping. It is more complicated than growing vegetables outdoors as you can get a number of crops per bed per year. You may plan a bed at a time and try your best to fit them in some sort of rotation in order to prevent a build up of soil-borne pests and diseases.

SOWING
Direct sowing into beds
The only crops I sow directly into the tunnel or greenhouse soil in January are early carrots (Namur F1 or Amsterdam Forcing) and early forcing type radishes (Short Top Forcing). I usually sow them at the very end of January but if it is very cold you should, of course, delay the sowing. The beds can be pre-warmed a couple of weeks beforehand by covering with black plastic which is removed

a couple of days before sowing. After sowing, the crop can be protected from the cold using a fleece. You can mix in a few radish seeds with the carrots. The radishes will quickly germinate and will indicate where the carrot row will be. This enables you to hoe between the rows.

Planting into beds

Towards the end of the month you can plant your first early chitted potatoes (Home Guard or Sharpe's Express). You can start chitting your potatoes in December. It's important that you have some fleece handy for covering up your emerging potato shoots to protect them from frosty spells.

In late January you can plant strawberries into your tunnel or greenhouse. The plants come from well-established runners from the previous year which were potted on and left outdoors until now. These will produce an extra early crop of delicious strawberries from April onwards.

Sowing into modules/pots (18–20°C)

Towards the end of January you can sow the following vegetables into modular trays and place them in your propagator or warm, south-facing windowsill in the house:

- Cabbage (Hispi F1 or Pyramid F1) – 1 seed per cell.
- Coriander (Leisure) – 5 seeds per cell.
- Chervil (Massa) – 5 seeds per cell.
- Dill (Dukat) – 5 seeds per cell.
- Leeks (Roxton F1) – 2 seeds per cell.
- Lettuce (various types) – 1–3 seeds per cell.
- Mangetout peas (Sweet Horizon) – 4 seeds per 7cm pots.
- Onions (Golden Bear F1) – 4 seeds per cell – for planting outside in April.
- Oriental salads (mizuna, rocket, tatsoi, etc.) – 5 seeds per cell.

- Scallions (Parade or Ishikura) – 5–10 seeds per cell, depending on how many you like in a bunch.

HARVESTING

Even in the coldest month of January you'll be able to harvest some healthy greens. You can get a wonderful salad bowl from the salads you have sown last September or October.

These include: salad rocket, wild rocket, various mustard leaves (Green Wave, Green in the snow, Red Frills, Green Frills), tatsoi, pak choi, corn salad, winter purslane, cress, mizuna, mibuna, komatsuna, texel greens, baby spinach, beet leaves (Bulls Blood) and possibly even some lettuce leaves.

GENERAL GREENHOUSE/POLYTUNNEL MAINTENANCE

- Clean and wash plastic or glass panes and all pots and trays.
- Replace cracked panes of glass and repair any rips in the plastic with special tape.
- Set up your heating bench or propagator.
- Keep the soil moist but not too wet.
- Ventilate on sunny days.
- You can pre-warm the soil by covering some empty beds with black plastic especially if you plan to direct sow an early crop.
- This is the best time to prune your grapevine (if you have one). Grapes can easily take over any tunnel or greenhouse, so be ruthless with the secateurs. Prune back all shoots from the last year and only leave a little stub with one or two buds on it. The new grapes will form on the new growth.
- If you haven't done so yet, clean your tools and rub boiled linseed oil onto the handles and a mixture of old oil and diesel to get rid of rust on metal blades.

FEBRUARY

In your greenhouse or tunnel you may now be fooled that spring has arrived. Your tunnel or greenhouse can easily warm up to 20°C during sunny spells. You also notice that the days are getting longer and your gardening itch is starting up again.

Anything you have missed from the January section can still be done now, it will be even safer. February is also the time to sow all your exciting warmth loving Mediterranean vegetables – tomatoes, peppers, chillies and aubergines.

SOWING
Direct sowing into beds
All throughout February you can sow the following vegetables directly into the beds:
- Beetroot (Pablo F1, Boltardy).
- Carrots (Namur F1, Amsterdam Forcing).
- Oriental brassica salads (various types).
- Peas, Mangetout (Sweet Horizon).
- Radish (Short Top Forcing) – small quantities at regular intervals.
- Turnips (Milan Purple Top) – small quantities at regular intervals.

Planting into beds
Throughout the month you can still plant the first early chitted potatoes (Home Guard or Sharpe's Express). Don't forget to cover the shoots with fleece during frosty weather.

You can also still plant early strawberries into your tunnel or greenhouse.

Early spring planted garlic can be planted now.

Sowing into modules/pots (18–20°C)
In February you can sow the following vegetables into modular

trays and place them in your propagator or warm, south-facing windowsill in the house:

- Aubergine (Black Prince F1) – 5 seeds per 7cm pot, for pricking out.
- Cabbage (Hispi F1 or Pyramid F1) – 1 seed per cell.
- Calabrese (Green Magic F1) – 1 seed per cell.
- Cauliflower (for mini cauliflowers) – 1 seed per cell.
- Celery (Victoria F1) – broadcast in a tray for pricking out later.
- Chilli peppers (various varieties) – 5 seeds per 7cm pot.
- Coriander, Dill and Chervil – 5 seeds per cell.
- Kohlrabi (Azur Star) – 1 seed per cell.
- Leeks (Roxton F1) – 2 seeds per cell.
- Lettuce (various types) – 1–3 seeds per cell.
- Mangetout peas (Sweet Horizon) – 4 seeds per 7cm pots.
- Onions (Golden Bear F1) – 4 seeds per cell.
- Oriental salads (mizuna, rocket, tatsoi, etc.) – 5 seeds per cell.
- Pepper (Roberta F1, Bell Boy F1) – 5 seeds per 7cm pot, for pricking out.
- Perpetual spinach and Swiss Chard – 1 seed per cell.
- Scallions (Parade or Ishikura) – 5–10 seeds per cell, depending on how many you like in a bunch.
- Tomato (Sungold F1 and others) – 5 seeds per 7cm pot, for pricking out.

HARVESTING

As the daylength increases in February your overwintering salads are starting to come into their own. You may even have a glut and enough for the whole neighbourhood. The overwintered perpetual spinach and Swiss chard are also cropping well now.

You can harvest:

Salad rocket, wild rocket, various mustard leaves (Green Wave, Green in the snow, Red Frills, Green Frills), tatsoi, pak choi, corn salad, winter purslane, cress, mizuna, mibuna, komatsuna, texel greens, baby spinach, beet leaves (Bulls Blood) and possibly even some lettuce leaves.

GENERAL GREENHOUSE/POLYTUNNEL MAINTENANCE
- Water lightly, once per week.
- Ventilate as much as possible.
- Continue planning. The more organized you are, the less work there will be later.
- It's a good time to dig in well-rotted manure or compost into empty beds. Remember that each bed needs to be fed every year. Do not manure the carrot bed – it's better to do it after the carrots are harvested.
- Cover up the emerging potato shoots with fleece or cover completely with soil if frost is forecast.
- Clean and wash plastic or glass and all pots and trays if you haven't done so earlier.
- Replace cracked panes of glass and repair any rips in the plastic with special tape.
- Set up your heating bench and replace the sand.
- You can pre-warm the soil by covering some empty beds with black plastic especially if you plan to direct sow an early crop.

MARCH

You will really feel the warmth in your greenhouse or polytunnel now and so will your plants. They will start to grow quite rapidly but be aware that the nights are still quite cold and there is still a high risk of frost. Many garden centres will try and sell you tomato plants from the end of March onwards. Don't let them tempt you until May.

SOWING
Direct sowing into beds
In March you can still sow the following vegetables directly into the soil. However, if you sow carrots, beetroot and peas now they will only be ready in mid June which is far too late to plant your tomatoes or peppers.

- Beetroot (Pablo F1).
- Carrots (Namur F1, Amsterdam Forcing).
- French beans (dwarf and climbing types).
- Peas, Mangetout (Sweet Horizon).
- Radish (Short Top Forcing) – small amounts at regular intervals.
- Turnips (Milan Purple Top) – small amounts at regular intervals.

Planting into beds
You can now plant out the seedlings you raised earlier on your heating bench: lettuce, scallions, dill, coriander, chervil, early cabbage, calabrese, mini cauliflowers, early leeks, perpetual spinach, Swiss chard, salad rocket and all other oriental salads. Most seedlings take about 4–5 weeks from sowing until they are ready to plant.

Sowing into modules/pots (18–20°C)
Do not let your heating bench clutter up too much. Most vegetables only require some warmth for germination and in March

the seedlings are better off if placed on a non-heated bench in the tunnel or greenhouse. Only your tomatoes, peppers, chillies, aubergines, courgettes, cucumbers, squash, pumpkins, celery, celeriac and basil should remain on the heating bench until they are planted in May. All other vegetables should be moved off the heating bench about a week after they have germinated.

In March you can sow the following vegetables into modular trays and place them in your propagator or warm, south-facing windowsill in the house:

- Aubergine (Black Prince F1) – 5 seeds per 7cm pot, for pricking out.
- Basil (Sweet Genovese) – 4 seeds per cell (only late in the month).
- Calabrese (Green Magic F1) – 1 seed per cell.
- Cauliflower (for mini cauliflowers) – 1 seed per cell.
- Celery (Victoria F1) – broadcast in a tray for pricking out later.
- Chilli peppers (various varieties) – 5 seeds per 7cm pot – only early in the month.
- Courgette (Parthenon) – 1 seed per 7cm pot.
- Coriander, Dill and Chervil – 5 seeds per cell.
- French beans (climbing and dwarf) – 5 seeds per 9cm pot.
- Kohlrabi (Azur Star) – 1 seed per cell.
- Lettuce (various types) – 1–3 seeds per cell.
- Oriental salads (mizuna, rocket, tatsoi, etc.) – 5 seeds per cell.
- Pepper (Roberta F1, Bell Boy F1) – 5 seeds per 7cm pot, for pricking out.
- Scallions (Parade or Ishikura) – 5–10 seeds per cell, depending on how many you like in a bunch.
- Tomato (Sungold F1 and others) – 5 seeds per 7cm pot, for pricking out.

Do not sow your cucumbers and melons yet. You'll get much better results if you wait until April to sow them.

For planting outside

You can also raise the following vegetables indoors for planting out into your vegetable garden later.

- Cabbage (early varieties) – 1 seed per cell.
- Calabrese (Green Magic F1) – 1 seed per cell.
- Celery (Victoria F1) – broadcast in a tray for pricking out later.
- Celeriac (Giant Prague) – broadcast in a tray for pricking out later.
- Kohlrabi (Azur Star) – 1 seed per cell.
- Leeks (Hannibal) – 2 seeds per cell.
- Lettuce (various) – 1–3 seeds per cell.
- Onions (Golden Bear F1) – 4 seeds per cell.
- Scallions (Ishikura Bunching) – 10 seeds per cell.

HARVESTING

Salad rocket, wild rocket, various mustard leaves (Green Wave, Green in the snow, Red Frills, Green Frills), tatsoi, pak choi, corn salad, winter purslane, cress, mizuna, mibuna, komatsuna, texel greens, baby spinach, beet leaves (Bulls Blood) and possibly even some lettuce leaves.

You can still harvest the overwintered Swiss chard and perpetual spinach and towards the end of the month you should get your first radishes and baby turnips.

GENERAL GREENHOUSE/POLYTUNNEL JOBS

- Water more frequently now, about twice a week. Do not saturate beds though.
- Ventilate as much as possible, but still close the doors and windows at night.
- Prick out aubergine, pepper and tomato seedlings into individual 7cm pots using good potting compost.
- Cover up the emerging potato shoots with fleece or cover completely with soil if frost is forecast.

- Continue with digging in well-rotted manure or compost into empty beds. Remember that each bed needs to be fed every year.
- Keep a watch out for pests, especially aphids, on a variety of crops and leatherjackets and cutworms on newly planted lettuce.
- Prick out celery seedlings into cell trays – one seedling per cell.
- Earth up potatoes and still watch out for frost. If frost is forecast you can either completely cover the potato stems with soil or compost or alternatively cover them with a double layer of fleece.

APRIL

April is one of the busiest months and one filled with immense responsibility. All your crops are now sown and you care for them as if they are your little babies. You certainly can't book a holiday during April because your seedlings in trays need to be watered every day and possibly twice if it's hot.

SOWING

Direct sowing into beds

You can sow radishes and baby turnips directly into the beds if there is space available.

Planting into beds

You can now plant out the seedlings you raised earlier on your heating bench: calabrese, mini cauliflowers, celery, chervil, coriander, courgette, dill, French beans, kohlrabi, lettuce, oriental salads and scallions.

Sowing into modules/pots (18–20°C)

In April you can sow the following vegetables into modular trays and place them in your propagator or warm, south-facing windowsill in the house:

- Basil (Sweet Genovese) – 4 seeds per cell.
- Celery (Victoria F1) – broadcast in a tray for pricking out later.
- Courgette (Defender F1) – 1 seed per 7cm pot.
- Cucumber (Passandra F1 and Styx F1) – 1 seed per 7cm pot.
- Coriander, Dill and Chervil – 5 seeds per cell.
- French beans (climbing and dwarf) – 5 seeds per 9cm pot.
- Kohlrabi (Azur Star) – 1 seed per cell.
- Lettuce (various types) – 1–3 seeds per cell.
- Melon (Emir F1) – 1 seed per 7cm pot.

- Sweetcorn (Sweet Nugget F1) – 1 seed per 7cm pot.

For planting outside
You can also raise the following vegetables indoors for planting out into your vegetable garden later: Brussels sprouts, cabbage, calabrese, cauliflower, chard, chervil, coriander, courgette, dill, endive, kale, kohlrabi, leeks, lettuce, parsley, perpetual spinach, pumpkins, scallions, squash, swede and turnip.

HARVESTING
In April you'll get your first rewards from your tunnel or greenhouse. You'll be harvesting a whole range of exciting, delicious and healthy crops: early Hispi cabbage, lots of lettuce, radish, scallions, baby turnips, kohlrabi, salad rocket and other oriental salads, spinach, chard, strawberries and even some baby potatoes.

GENERAL GREENHOUSE/POLYTUNNEL JOBS
- Water more frequently now.
- Ventilate as much as possible.
- Prick out celery and celeriac seedlings into modular trays.
- Pot on aubergines, peppers and tomatoes into 10cm pots using good potting compost.
- Most of the overwintered crops (oriental salads, spinach and chard) will have bolted by now and should be pulled.
- Keep a watch out for pests, especially aphids on a variety of crops and leatherjackets and cutworms on newly planted lettuce.
- Spray aphid-susceptible plants with a garlic spray every 10 days.
- Prick out and pot on plants as necessary.
- Towards the end of the month lower the temperature of your propagator to 15°C to harden off your tomatoes, peppers etc. before planting them into the beds next month.

MAY

May is the most exciting month in your tunnel or greenhouse. This is the time to plant out your summer crops – your tomatoes, peppers, aubergines, cucumbers and basil. Take good care of them and give them a fabulous soil and they will reward you with a bounty of delicious sun-ripened fruit. Once the busy spell of planting is over you can start to relax again.

PLANTING INTO BEDS

You will appreciate now all the hard work of preparing the beds in the previous months. There is no shortcut: only a well-prepared and well-fertilized bed can sustain the demands of the heavy yielding summer crops.

All your summer crops can be planted now:
- Aubergines
- Basil
- Courgette
- Cucumbers
- Melons (only in warm districts)
- Peppers and chillies
- Tomatoes
- You can also plant out into the tunnel or greenhouse the seedlings you sowed last month on your heating bench: French beans, celery, lettuce, scallions, dill, coriander and chervil.

SOWING
Sowing into modules/pots (18–20°C)

In May you can sow the following vegetables into modular trays or pots and place them in your propagator or warm, south-facing windowsill in the house:
- Basil (Sweet Genovese) – 4 seeds per cell.

- Celery (Victoria F1) – broadcast in a tray for pricking out later.
- Courgette (Defender F1) – 1 seed per 7cm pot.
- Cucumber (Passandra F1 and Styx F1) – 1 seed per 7cm pot.
- Coriander, Dill and Chervil – 5 seeds per cell each.
- French beans (climbing and dwarf) – 5 seeds per 9cm pot.
- Florence fennel (Rondo F1) – 1 seed per cell.
- Lettuce (various types) – 1–3 seeds per cell.
- Melon (Emir F1) – 1 seed per 7cm pot.
- Sweetcorn – 1 seed per small pot.

For planting outside
You can raise the following vegetables indoors for planting out into your vegetable garden later:

Brussels sprouts, coriander, chervil, cabbage, cauliflower, calabrese, courgette, dill, kale, kohlrabi, lettuce, pumpkins, spring leeks, scallions and squash.

HARVESTING
In May you will be so grateful for having a tunnel or greenhouse. There is very little ready from your vegetable garden and you work so hard at it, but at least indoors you'll get a great range of fresh and wonderful vegetables and salads.

You can harvest: beetroot, early Hispi cabbage, calabrese, cauliflower (mini), carrots, dill, coriander, chervil, leeks for bunching, kohlrabi, lettuce, peas, potatoes, radish, scallions, salad rocket and other oriental salads, spinach, Swiss chard, strawberries and baby turnips.

GENERAL GREENHOUSE/POLYTUNNEL MAINTENANCE
- Water more frequently and more heavily now.
- Ventilate as much as possible.
- Dig out potatoes and early cabbages to make room for summer crops.

- Keep a watch out for pests, especially slugs and snails on newly planted salads, aphids on a variety of crops and fleabeetles on brassica salads.
- Spray aphid-susceptible plants with a garlic spray every 7–10 days.
- Prick out and pot on plants as necessary.
- Harden off your summer crops that are nearly ready for planting (tomatoes, peppers, aubergines, cucumber, melons, peppers) by taking them off the propagator.
- If you haven't fed the beds for the summer crops, do so now.

JUNE

June is one of my favourite months in the tunnel or greenhouse. The majority of crops are planted by now and the responsibility of watering your seedlings every day is nearly over. You can enjoy tending your crops and observe how they develop. There is also a relatively decent range of crops ready to harvest.

SOWING
Direct sowing into beds
In June your tunnel or greenhouse is most likely to be full of crops and there is no space for sowing crops direct. Generally you'll be much better off raising plants in modular trays as you gain at least 4 weeks of valuable growing space.

Planting into beds
You can still plant out all your summer crops such as tomatoes, peppers, chillies, aubergines, basil, courgettes, cucumbers, melons and sweetcorn, especially if you have well-established plants. Even if it is on the late side for some of these crops you will still get a decent yield from them.

Sowing into modules/pots (18–20°C)
You can still sow a range of crops into modular trays. There will always be crops harvested, beds cleared and space available. So even if your tunnel or greenhouse is full at present there will be space in 4–6 weeks when your new transplants are ready to plant.

For planting inside
- Basil (Sweet Genovese) – 4 seeds per cell.
- Chinese cabbage (Yuki F1) – 1 seed per cell.
- Courgette (Defender F1) – 1 seed per 7cm pot.

- Cucumber (Passandra F1 and Styx F1) – 1 seed per 7cm pot.
- Coriander, Dill and Chervil – 5 seeds per cell.
- French beans (climbing and dwarf) – 5 seeds per 9cm pot.
- Florence fennel (Rondo F1) – 1 seed per cell.
- Lettuce (various types) – 1–3 seeds per cell.
- Pak Choi (Joi Choi) – 1 seed per cell.
- Parsley (curly and flat leaf) – 4 seeds per cell.
- Scallions (Ishikura Bunching) – 10 seeds per cell.

For planting outside
There are still a few crops that can be raised indoors for planting outside about 4 weeks later: Brussels sprouts, coriander, chervil, cabbage, cauliflower, calabrese, Chinese cabbage, dill, Florence fennel, kale, kohlrabi, lettuce and scallions.

HARVESTING
In June you will get a lot of produce from your tunnel or greenhouse: beetroot, cabbage, carrots, chervil, coriander, courgette, dill, French beans, kohlrabi, lettuce, peas, potatoes, radish, salads (any), scallions, spinach, strawberries and turnips.

If you are lucky enough and live in a favourable area you may already get some tomatoes and cucumbers. Unfortunately my tomatoes only start to ripen from July onwards.

GENERAL GREENHOUSE/POLYTUNNEL MAINTENANCE
- Water more frequently and more heavily now, probably about two to three times per week.
- Ventilate as much as possible.
- Weekly maintenance for summer crops: side-shooting and training tomatoes, cucumbers and melons. You should also remove the lower discoloured or diseased leaves.
- Spray aphid-susceptible plants with a garlic spray every 7–10 days.

- Keep a watch out for pests, especially whitefly on tomatoes, aphids on salads and fleabeetle on brassica salads.
- Remove weeds as otherwise they will compete with your plants.
- Prick out and pot on plants as necessary.

JULY

Your tunnel or greenhouse is absolutely packed and you'll be harvesting fruits from your summer crops – the first tomato of the year is always the most anticipated and delicious. Soon you'll have more food than you can cope with. All the other summer crops (cucumbers, peppers, aubergines etc.) are also starting to produce.

SOWING

Direct sowing into beds

There shouldn't be any empty space in your tunnel or greenhouse for direct sowing.

Planting into beds

You can plant all the crops you have sown a month earlier in modular trays into your tunnel or greenhouse: basil, Chinese cabbage, coriander, dill and chervil, courgette, cucumber, French beans, Florence fennel, lettuce, pak choi, parsley, scallions.

Sowing into modules/pots (18–20°C)

It's surprising how many crops you can sow in July for planting into the tunnel or greenhouse about 4–6 weeks later.

For planting inside

- Basil (Sweet Genovese) – 4 seeds per cell.
- Calabrese (Green Magic F1) – 1 seed per cell.
- Chinese cabbage (Yuki F1) – 1 seed per cell.
- Claytonia (or Winter Purslane) – 5 seeds per cell.
- Chervil, Coriander, Dill – 5 seeds per cell each.
- French beans (climbing and dwarf) – 5 seeds per 9cm pot.
- Florence fennel (Rondo F1) – 1 seed per cell.

- Lettuce (various types) – 1–3 seeds per cell.
- Oriental brassica salads (all types) – 5 seeds per cell.
- Pak Choi (various) – 1 seed per cell.
- Parsley (curly and flat leaf) – 4 seeds per cell.
- Scallions (Ishikura Bunching) – 10 seeds per cell.

For planting outside
There are only a few crops that can be sown indoors in modular trays for planting out later: Chinese cabbage, coriander, chervil, dill, Florence fennel, lettuce, oriental brassica salads (rocket, mizuna, mustards etc), pak choi and scallions.

HARVESTING
In July you'll discover how worthwhile it is to have a tunnel or greenhouse. Hopefully you are not away on holiday otherwise your neighbours or friends will enjoy your bounty in exchange for a little bit of watering.

It is very important to harvest your crops regularly. You should harvest your courgettes and cucumbers at least twice per week and your tomatoes, peppers and aubergines at least once per week. If you don't, the plants often get exhausted and diseased.

You can harvest: aubergines, basil, chillies, coriander, courgette, cucumber, dill, Florence fennel, French beans, lettuce, melons, pak choi, parsley, peppers, salads, scallions, spinach and tomatoes.

GENERAL GREENHOUSE/POLYTUNNEL MAINTENANCE
- Water more frequently and more heavily now, probably about three times per week, especially during hot spells.
- Ventilate as much as possible. The tunnel and greenhouse doors should be left open until late in the evening or even throughout the night. Ensure that they are secure.
- Weekly maintenance for summer crops: side-shooting and

training tomatoes, cucumbers and melons. You should also remove the lower discoloured or diseased leaves.

- Harvest regularly when the crops are ready and not necessarily when you would like them.
- Keep a look out for pests, especially greenhouse whitefly, aphids, red spider mite, slugs and snails.
- Keep weeds down. They compete with your plants and create a damp atmosphere. This reduces the air-flow between plants and fungal diseases thrive in these conditions.
- Spray aphid susceptible plants with a garlic spray every 7 days.

AUGUST

In August there is even more bounty than in July and you reap the rewards for all your efforts. You may even have produced enough courgettes and cucumbers for the whole neighbourhood. The tomatoes can be made into soups and frozen. Be aware though that in August there is often an influx of pests and diseases. Often you are too busy harvesting your crops and somewhat neglect your plants. It is important to keep a close eye on your plants during this month.

SOWING

Direct sowing into beds

It is very unlikely that you will find any empty space in your tunnel or greenhouse for direct sowing.

Planting into beds

You can plant all the crops you have sown a month earlier in modular trays into your tunnel or greenhouse: calabrese, Chinese cabbage, claytonia, coriander, dill and chervil, Florence fennel, lettuce, oriental brassica salads, pak choi, parsley and scallions.

Sowing into modules/pots (18–20°C)
For planting inside

- Calabrese (Green Magic F1) – 1 seed per cell.
- Chard (any type) – 1 seed per cell.
- Chinese cabbage (Yuki F1) – 1 seed per cell.
- Claytonia (or Winter Purslane) – 5 seeds per cell.
- Chervil, Coriander, Dill – 5 seeds per cell each.
- Florence fennel (Rondo F1) – 1 seed per cell.
- Lettuce (various types) – 1–3 seeds per cell.
- Oriental brassica salads (all types) – 5 seeds per cell.

- Pak Choi (various) – 1 seed per cell.
- Parsley (curly and flat leaf) – 4 seeds per cell.
- Scallions (Ishikura Bunching) – 10 seeds per cell.
- Spinach (annual) – 4 seeds per cell.
- Spinach (perpetual) – 1 seed per cell.

For planting outside
There are only a few crops that can be sown indoors in modular trays for planting out later: coriander, chervil, dill, Florence fennel, lettuce, oriental brassica salads (rocket, mizuna, mustards etc), pak choi and scallions.

HARVESTING
In August you are bound to have plenty of excess produce. You have the choice to preserve, to give away or to compost, so be prepared for the glut and warn your friends and neighbours about those courgettes or, worse even, marrows.

Harvest your courgettes and cucumbers at least twice per week and your tomatoes, peppers and aubergines at least once per week.

You can harvest: aubergines, basil, coriander, Chinese cabbage, chillies, courgette, cucumber, dill, Florence fennel, French beans, lettuce, melons, pak choi, peppers, salads, scallions, spinach and tomatoes.

GENERAL GREENHOUSE/POLYTUNNEL MAINTENANCE
- Water more frequently and more heavily now, about two to three times per week, especially during hot spells. Avoid watering in the evening as this will encourage the spread of fungal diseases.
- Ventilate as much as possible. The tunnel and greenhouse doors should be left open until late in the evening or even throughout the night.
- Weekly maintenance for summer crops: side-shooting and training tomatoes, cucumbers and melons. You should also remove the lower discoloured or diseased leaves.

- During August it is most important to check your plants regularly and remove any dead or diseased plants or plant parts, especially for grey mould (botrytis) on tomatoes and many other plants as well as keeping a check on the greenhouse whitefly.
- Harvest regularly when the crops are ready (not as and when you'd like them).
- Keep a watch out for pests, especially greenhouse whitefly, tomato moth caterpillars, aphids, red spider mite, slugs and snails.
- Spray aphid susceptible plants with a garlic spray every 7 days.

SEPTEMBER

Your tunnel or greenhouse is likely to get a little bit out of hand during this month, with most crops no longer at their prime. Pests and diseases are also spreading much faster than before. You have to decide which plants to clear and which ones to leave a bit longer. Remember it's a good idea to clear some areas to let some light and air in for the remaining plants. A good excuse is that you need that space for your winter salads.

Many commercial growers claim that they get a much better income from winter salads than from a tomato crop in the summer.

SOWING
In September you can sow a whole range of excellent winter salads that will provide you with fresh greens throughout the winter until the following spring if they are well looked after.

Direct sowing into beds
There is likely to be space available again for sowing directly into the beds. Any salad crop can be sown directly into the ground now or sown into modular trays for planting out later. The decision is yours. You can also get an excellent crop of radishes and baby turnips from a direct sowing in September.

Planting into beds
All the crops that have been raised in modular trays in the previous month can now be planted out into the tunnel or greenhouse: calabrese, chard, Chinese cabbage, claytonia, chervil, coriander, dill, Florence fennel, lettuce, oriental brassica salads, pak choi, parsley, scallions, spinach (annual and perpetual).

Sowing into modules/pots (18–20°C)
- Claytonia (or Winter Purslane) – 5 seeds per cell.
- Chervil, Coriander, Dill – 5 seeds per cell each.
- Lettuce (winter types) – 1–3 seeds per cell.
- Oriental brassica salads (all types) – 5 seeds per cell.
- Pak Choi (various) – 1 seed per cell.
- Scallions (Ishikura Bunching) – 10 seeds per cell.
- Spinach (annual) – 4 seeds per cell.
- Spinach (perpetual) – 1 seed per cell.

HARVESTING
September is still a very productive month in your tunnel or greenhouse.

You can harvest: aubergines, basil, calabrese, coriander, Chinese cabbage, courgette, cucumber, dill, Florence fennel, French beans, lettuce, melons, oriental brassica salads, pak choi, parsley, peppers, salads, scallions, spinach, tomatoes.

GENERAL GREENHOUSE/POLYTUNNEL MAINTENANCE
- Water less frequently and less heavily now, about once or twice per week. Avoid watering in the evening as this will encourage the spread of fungal diseases.
- Ventilate as much as possible. The tunnel and greenhouse doors should be left open during the day (unless it's stormy) and closed at night.
- Weekly maintenance for summer crops: side-shooting and training tomatoes, cucumbers and melons. Remove the lower leaves that are discoloured or diseased.
- Check all plants regularly and remove dead and diseased plants and plant parts.
- Keep a watch out for pests, especially greenhouse whitefly, tomato moth caterpillars, aphids, red spider mite, slugs and snails.
- Harvest regularly when the crops are ready.

OCTOBER

October is the month for clearing and tidying. Your cucumbers and courgettes are likely to be finished and many other plants are getting exhausted and diseased, but hopefully you have a batch of new salad crops ready to plant out now. I always enjoy this time of year because the tunnel or greenhouse becomes completely transformed and rejuvenated again.

SOWING
Direct sowing into beds
There is now plenty of space again for sowing directly into the beds. Any salad crop can be sown directly into the ground now or sown into modules for planting out later. The decision is yours.

Planting into beds
I always look forward to planting out the garlic cloves into the beds in October. If you plant them in early October they will be ready and harvested in May just in time before your tomatoes need to be planted. You can also plant overwintering onion sets.

Sowing into modules/pots (18–20°C)
The best time for your overwintering salads was really in September, but if you have missed that date you can still sow them now. They may not be ready before the end of the year but will produce well in late winter until early spring.
- Claytonia (or Winter Purslane) – 5 seeds per cell.
- Chervil, Coriander, Dill – 5 seeds per cell each.
- Oriental brassica salads (all types) – 5 seeds per cell.
- Scallions (Ishikura Bunching) – 10 seeds per cell.
- Spinach (annual) – 4 seeds per cell.

HARVESTING

In October the summer crops are fizzling out and their quality declines.

You may still harvest some: aubergines, basil, calabrese, coriander, Chinese cabbage, courgette, cucumber, dill, Florence fennel, French beans, lettuce, melons, oriental brassica salads, pak choi, parsley, peppers, salads, scallions, spinach and tomatoes.

GENERAL GREENHOUSE/POLYTUNNEL MAINTENANCE

- Water even less now. Once a week should be sufficient. Only water in the morning.
- Ventilate as much as possible. The tunnel and greenhouse doors should be left open during the day (unless it's stormy) and closed at night.
- Remove all tomato leaves to encourage ripening of the remaining green tomatoes.
- Keep a watch out for pests, especially slugs and snails on your newly planted salads.
- Clear plants that have finished cropping.

NOVEMBER

We usually don't think about our tunnel or greenhouse in November. There is very little need for it especially if you have planted the winter salads and overwintering garlic cloves and onion sets in October. There is much less need for watering and also the weeds have slowed down. Nevertheless the most important job is ventilation. Any chance you get you should open the doors.

SOWING
Direct sowing into beds
I rarely sow crops at this time of year. The reason is that I just want to have a break but it is possible to sow early carrots and early peas now. They will germinate and remain quite small throughout December and January and then start to grow quickly. Some gardeners sow broad beans in their tunnel or greenhouse in November. I tried it a couple of times but I always preferred the outdoor crop that was planted at the same time.

Planting into beds
You can still plant garlic cloves directly into the beds. They will be ready in June.

Sowing into modules/pots (18–20°C)
If you still haven't sown your winter salads you can sow them now, but they may only start to crop in early spring.
- Claytonia (or Winter Purslane) – 5 seeds per cell.
- Chervil, Coriander, Dill – 5 seeds per cell each.
- Oriental brassica salads (all types) – 5 seeds per cell.
- Spinach (annual) – 4 seeds per cell.

HARVESTING

In November all your summer crops are coming to an end with a possible exception of tomatoes that can go on forever in a mild winter.

You may still harvest some: calabrese, coriander, corn salad, dill, Florence fennel, lettuce, oriental brassica salads, pak choi, parsley, radish, salads, scallions, spinach, tomatoes and turnip.

GENERAL GREENHOUSE/POLYTUNNEL MAINTENANCE

- Hardly water at all – once a week at the most. Only water in the morning.
- Ventilate as much as possible. The tunnel and greenhouse doors should be opened during the day (weather permitting) and closed at night.
- Clear plants that have finished cropping.
- Harvest and weed your winter salads properly.
- Start preparing the soil for the early spring crops by incorporating compost or composted manure into the soil.

DECEMBER

It's a good time to take a break from your tunnel or greenhouse. All you need to do is harvest your salads and ventilate as much as possible. If you have spare time you can prepare the beds for the following year. It's a good idea to let the beds settle in for a while before sowing and planting again.

Take time to reflect on the gardening year and repeat what went well and find out what went wrong with other crops and make improvements or changes.

SOWING
Personally I think it's best not to sow anything in December and instead wait until January when the days are starting to get longer again.

HARVESTING
You may still harvest some: coriander, corn salad, dill, lettuce, oriental brassica salads, pak choi, parsley, radish, scallions, spinach and turnip.

GENERAL GREENHOUSE/POLYTUNNEL MAINTENANCE
- Hardly water at all – once a week at the most.
- Ventilate as much as possible.
- Clear all remaining summer crops. Don't leave any of their crop residues in your tunnel or greenhouse otherwise their relevant pests and diseases will be carried over to the new crops.
- Start chitting your first early potatoes indoors.
- Continue harvesting your winter salads.
- Prepare the soil for the early spring crops by incorporating compost or composted manure into the soil.

- Tidy and clean the tunnel or greenhouse: wash the plastic or glass, clean and tidy away the pots and trays.
- Clean your tools and rub boiled linseed oil onto the handles and a mixture of old oil and diesel to get rid of rust on metal blades.
- Order your seeds, seed potatoes, onion sets and garlic bulbs.

VEGETABLE CROP SUMMARY

Vegetable	Variety	Sowing Dates	Propagation	Spacing	Planting details	Sowing to harvesting	Duration of season
Aubergine	Black Beauty, Black Prince F1	Sow in early March at 20°C	Sow in seed trays and prick out into 7cm pots when first true leaf appears	45cm x 45cm	May need simple support (cane)	20 weeks	Harvest weekly from July to October
Bean, French (dwarf)	Purple Teepee, Safari	Sow from late March to late June	For early crops sow indoors in small pots, later sow direct into the ground	25cm x 25cm		12 weeks	May to late September
Bean, French (climbing)	Eva, Cobra	Sow from late March to June	For early crops sow indoors in small pots, later sow direct into the ground	20cm x 40cm	Needs to be trained up canes or string	15 weeks	June–October
Bean, Runner	Enorma, Lady Di	Sow from late March to June	For early crops sow indoors in small pots, later sow direct into the ground	20cm x 40cm	Needs to be trained up canes or string	16 weeks	June–October
Beetroot	Pablo F1	1. February 2. March	Normally sown direct into the ground about 2cm deep	23cm x 8cm or 15cm x 15cm	Beetroot seeds are clusters of seeds, so they need to be thinned as early as possible	Earlies: 8–10 weeks	1. May 2. June

Vegetable	Variety	Sowing Dates	Propagation	Spacing	Planting details	Sowing to harvesting	Duration of season
Cabbage, Chinese	Yuki F1	Late May until late July	For early sowings a bolt-resistant cultivar is required	30cm x 30cm	Keep soil moist at all times. For succession sow a small quantity every 2 weeks	10 weeks	July until October
Cabbage, Spring	Hispi F1	Late January until March	Sow in modules and plant out into tunnel 4 weeks later	30cm x 30cm	In cold areas protect with cloches	12–16 weeks	April–May
Calabrese	Fiesta F1, Green Magic F1	1. Feb–March 2. July	Sow in modules at 15°C	35cm x 35cm	After cutting the central head many side-shoots can be harvested over the following weeks	10–15 weeks	1. May 2. September
Carrots, early	Amsterdam Forcing, Early Nantes, Namur F1	Late January until March	Seeds are sown direct into the ground	15cm x 5cm or 20cm x 4cm	Never attempt to transplant carrots as they will fork	14–20 weeks	May–June

Vegetable	Variety	Sowing Dates	Propagation	Spacing	Planting details	Sowing to harvesting	Duration of season
Cauliflower, early	Igor F1	Feb–March	Sow in modules and plant out into tunnel 4 weeks later	60cm x 50cm	Sow small quantities in 2 week intervals	16 weeks	May–June
Celery	Victoria, Lathom Blanching Galaxy	Late February until June	Broadcast seeds in pots without covering, then prick out into modular trays (1 seed/cell)	27cm x 27cm equidistant spacing in block formation	Keep plants well watered	16–20 weeks	May until November
Courgette	Defender F1, Ambassador F1, Partenon F1, Parador F1 (yellow)	Mid March until June	Plant in tunnel in late April. Plant in tunnel in late June	90cm apart	Protect from frost if necessary. Harvest regularly, at least twice a week in summer	10–14 weeks	June–Sept August–Nov
Cucumber	Choose all-female F1 hybrids Passandra F1, Styx F1	April until June	Sow in heating bench and pot on into 9cm pots and plant in tunnel mid May until early July	45cm apart	Train vertically along string or cane	15 weeks	Early July–Sept Late July–Oct
Endive	Pancalieri	Feb–March July–Aug	Plant in tunnel in late March to late April. Plant in tunnel in August to September	30cm x 30cm	Can be used as cut-and-come-again salad crop	14–16 weeks	May–June Sept–Nov

Vegetable	Variety	Sowing Dates	Propagation	Spacing	Planting details	Sowing to harvesting	Duration of season
Fennel, Florence	Romanesco, Rondo F1	Late April Mid June–July	Plant bolt-resistant variety in early June. Plant in tunnel in July–Aug	35cm x 35cm	Prefers to grow in the warmer part of the year	12–14 weeks	August Sept–Oct
Garlic	Solent White, Early Purple White	Plant in late September until November	Plant individual cloves	20cm x 30cm	Harvest when leaves turn yellow, before they fall over	24–38 weeks	May–June
Kohlrabi	Azur Star, Lanro	Feb–March June–July	Plant in tunnel in late March–early April Plant in tunnel in July–Aug	30cm x 30cm	It's important not to plant seedlings too deep otherwise the 'bulb' will rot	8–12 weeks	May Sept–Nov
Lettuce	Too many to list	Late January until August Feb–March	Sow individual seeds into modular trays and plant out 4 weeks later. Ensure that germination temperature is not above 25°C	25cm x 25cm	Sow at weekly or fortnightly intervals	12–14 weeks	March until November
Pea, Mangetout	Sweet Horizon		Sow in small pots or sow direct into the tunnel	Wice drill (10cm), sow seeds 7cm apart	Provide climbing support	14–16 weeks	Late April–July

Vegetable	Variety	Sowing Dates	Propagation	Spacing	Planting details	Sowing to harvesting	Duration of season
Pea, Sugar Snap	Garnet	Nov or Feb–March	Sow in small pots or sow direct into the tunnel	Wide drill (10cm), sow seeds 7cm apart	Provide climbing support	14–16 weeks	Late April–July
Pepper (sweet)	Bendigo F1, Bell Boy F1	Sow in February at 20°C, then pot on later	Plant in tunnel in May	45cm each way in a double row per bed	Sometimes simple staking is required	24–26 weeks	Harvest from late July–Oct
Pepper (chilli)	Demon Red, Ring of Fire, Navaho, Hungarian Wax	Sow in February at 20°C, then pot on into 9cm pots	Plant in tunnel in May	45cm each way in a double row per bed	Sometimes simple staking is required	24–26 weeks	Harvest from late July–Oct
Potatoes (early)	Homeguard, Orla, Sharpe's Express	Late January until early March	Plant chitted tubers in tunnel	30cm in rows 50cm apart	Earthing up, Frost protection is required	12–16 weeks	May–June
Radish early	Short Top Forcing	Feb–March Aug–Sept	Sow direct in tunnel	10cm in rows 25cm apart	Make successional sowings	4–6 weeks	March–April Sept–Oct

Vegetable	Variety	Sowing Dates	Propagation	Spacing	Planting details	Sowing to harvesting	Duration of season
Oriental Salads	Rocket, Mizuna, Tatsoi, Mustards, etc	1. Jan–March 2. Aug–Oct	Sow in modular trays (4 seeds/cell) at 15–18°C, plant in tunnel	20cm in rows 25cm apart	Harvest leaves regularly	4–8 weeks	1. March–May 2. Oct–April
Spinach, Annual	Firebird F1, Bella F1	1. Feb–April 2. Aug–Oct	Sow in modular trays (3 seeds/cell) or sow in situ in tunnel	10–15cm apart in rows 20–25cm apart	The closer the spacing the smaller the leaves	4–7 weeks	1. March–May 2. Oct–March
Spinach, Perpetual	No variety	1. Feb–March 2. September	1. Sow in modular trays (1 seed/cell), plant in tunnel. 2. Sow in modular trays, plant in tunnel or sow in situ.	30cm apart in rows 35cm apart	Each seed produces 3–5 seedlings which need thinning at propagation stage. Harvest regularly	15 weeks	1. Late March–May 2. Oct–March
Squash	Sunburst F1, Crown Prince F1, Delicata, Little Gem – Rolet	1. Mid March 2. Late May	1. Plant in tunnel late April 2. Plant in tunnel in late June	90cm apart	Protect from frost if necessary. Harvest regularly, at least twice a week during summer	10–14 weeks	1. June–Sept 2. Aug–Nov

Vegetable	Variety	Sowing Dates	Propagation	Spacing	Planting details	Sowing to harvesting	Duration of season
Sweetcorn	Golden Bantam, Black Aztec, Jubilee F1	Late March–April	Sow single seed in deep modular tray, plant in tunnel in early June	40cm apart in rows 60cm apart	To assist in pollination plant in blocks. Shake the plants to assist the pollination	15–20 weeks	Aug–Sept
Swiss Chard	Swiss Chard, Ruby Chard, Bright Lights	1. Feb–March 2. Sept	Sow in modular trays (1 seed/cell), plant in tunnel	30cm apart in rows 35cm apart	Each seed produces 3–5 seedlings which need thinning at propagation stage. Harvest regularly	15 weeks	1. Late March–May 2. Oct–March
Tomato	Sungold F1, Rosada F1, Tigerella, Shirley F1 Ferline	Late January until mid March	Sow in seed trays and prick out into small pots for growing in a tunnel. Plant in May	45cm apart each way (double row)	Staking and side-shooting necessary every week	20–22 weeks	July–Nov
Turnip	Milan Purple Top, White Globe	1. Feb–late March 2. Aug–early Sept	Sow in modular trays (1 seed/cell), plant in tunnel or sow in situ in tunnel	10cm apart in rows 25cm apart	Beware of flea-beetle attack in May/June on outdoor crops. Thin early to required spacing	8–12 weeks	1. April–June 2. Oct–Nov

GLOSSARY

Acid – A soil with a pH of below 7.

Aerobic – A process which takes place in the presence of air.

Alkaline – A soil with a pH of over 7.

Anaerobic – A process which takes place without air.

Annual – A plant that completes its lifecycle from seed to seed in one year.

Bare-rooted – A plant lifted from the soil as opposed to a potted plant.

Beneficial insect – An insect that preys on pests or diseases or assists in plant pollination.

Biennial – A plant that completes its lifecycle from seed to seed in a two-year period.

Biological control – A method of controlling pests by the introduction of a predator.

Blanching – In gardening terms it means to exclude light from the plants, either the whole plant or the leaves and stems.

Bolting – The premature production of flowers and seeds.

Broadcast – A sowing technique whereby seeds are scattered and raked into the soil.

Capping – A crust that forms on the surface of certain soils, often as a cause of compaction or heavy rainfall followed by quick drying.

Catch crop – A catch crop refers to a quick growing crop that is sown amongst slow growing vegetables to make the maximum use of space.

Clamp – A structure made of earth for storing root vegetables outdoors.

Cloche – A movable structure traditionally made of a metal frame and glass panes. Cloches nowadays come in many designs, mostly in plastic or netting.

Cold frame – A rectangular box with a glass or plastic lid used for propagation and hardening off.

Cotyledon – The first leaves produced by a seedling.

Deficiency – An adverse condition in plants that is caused by a shortage of one or more plant nutrients.

Direct sowing – Where seeds are sown directly into the open ground rather than raised indoors in trays or pots.

Disorder – An adverse condition in plants that is commonly caused by environmental factors.

Double digging – Method of digging to a depth of two spades without bringing the subsoil up to the surface.

Drill – A shallow trench or furrow in which seeds are sown.

Earthing up – To draw soil around the base of a plant for support, for increasing the growing space or for blanching purposes.

Erosion – The process of soil being washed away or blown off the surface of the ground.

F1 Hybrid – F1 refers to "first filial" or first generation offspring from two pure bred parents.

Foliar feeding – An application of liquid fertilizer to the plant foliage.

Friable – Describes a soil that is crumbly and capable of forming a tilth.

Genetic engineering – The mechanical transfer of DNA.

Germination – The development of a seed into a seedling.

Green manure – A crop which is grown with the purpose of improving the soil in terms of nutrient content and/or structure. A green manure crop is always incorporated where it has grown.

Half hardy – Plants that can tolerate low temperatures but not frost.

Hardy – Plants which can withstand frost without protection

Hardening off – To acclimatize plants gradually to cooler

conditions. This is especially important for plants that were raised in warm conditions.

Haulm – The leaves (foliage) of plants such as potatoes.

Herbicide – A weedkiller.

Hybrid – The offspring of a cross between two or more varieties, usually of the same species.

Humus – The fragrant, spongy, nutrient-rich material resulting from decomposition of organic matter.

Leaching – The downward washing and loss of soluble nutrients from the topsoil.

Legume – Vegetables of the *Leguminosae* family, e.g. peas and beans. They have the ability to take up nitrogen from the air.

Modules – Moulded trays which are divided up into individual cells. The cells are filled with seed compost and seeds can be sown individually and planted out with minimum soil disturbance.

Monogerm – A seed that produces a single plant. Beetroot and chard seeds are not monogerm so you will get a few seedlings from every seed unless you buy special monogerm seeds.

Mulch – A layer of an organic or inorganic material laid over the ground for the purpose of controlling weeds and protecting the soil surface.

Natural enemy – A creature or organism that preys upon another.

Nematode – A microscopic eelworm.

Nitrogen – One of the main plant nutrients. Used for the growth of leaves and shoots.

Nutrient – A plant food.

Open pollinated – A non-hybrid variety, one that can reproduce itself in kind.

Organic matter – A material which derives and consists of living organisms either dead or alive.

pH – The units by which the degree of acidity or alkalinity is measured.

Perennial – A non-woody plant that has a lifecycle of over three years. A herbaceous perennial dies back and becomes dormant in winter and grows again in the following spring.

Pesticide – A product that will kill pests, diseases or weeds.

Pheromone – A chemical substance which is secreted by animals and affects the behaviour of other animals.

Phosphate – A phosphorus compound (P_2O_5).

Phosphorus – Major plant nutrient, especially important for root growth.

Pinch out – To remove the growing tip of a plant to encourage branching.

Pollination – The transfer of pollen to the stigma of a flower to fertilize it.

Potash – A potassium compound (K_2O).

Potassium – Major plant nutrient especially important for flower and fruit development.

Predator – An animal that eats other animals.

Prick out – To transfer seedlings from a seed tray into a pot or seedbed.

Resistance – Resistance implies that a variety of vegetable will resist disease when exposed to a disease-causing pathogen such as a fungus, bacteria or virus.

Rotation – A system where crops are grouped into plant families and grown in different plots on a 3–4 year cycle. This limits the build up of soil-borne pests and diseases and makes the best use of soil nutrients.

Rotavator – A machine with rotating blades which break up the soil.

Soil conditioner – Material that improves the structure of a soil.

Spore – The reproductive body of a fungus.

Subsoil – The soil layer below the topsoil also called B-horizon.

Tap root – A strong growing, vertical root as in carrot or dandelion.

Tilth – The fine, crumbly structure on the soil surface.

Tolerance – Tolerance implies that a variety of vegetable will perform relatively well when exposed to environmental stresses such as cold weather, hot weather or drought.

Top-dressing – An application of a layer of organic matter onto the soil surface.

Trace elements – A plant nutrient which plants require in very small quantities.

Variety – A genetically similar population of plants, distinct in one or more traits from other populations.

Water table – The level of the soil below which the soil is saturated by ground water.

ACKNOWLEDGEMENTS

Many thanks to my children Julian, Christopher, Isabella, Anna-Maya, Thien and Elsbeth for their patience and all the endless cups of tea while writing this book.

I'm most grateful to Ray Warner from Thomas Etty Heritage Seed Company who kindly gave permission to use his wonderful Victorian images.

Many thanks to Margaret Holland for proof reading the text and Dympna O'Driscoll for her excellent illustrations.

This book would not have been possible without my wonderful wife Joanna who really made it all happen. Thank you.

This book is dedicated to my mother Iris who instilled in me a love of gardening from a young age. Our garden was my playground, dining-room, workroom and on summer nights my bedroom under the stars. From when I was eight years old I dug over my mother's garden in Germany, winter after winter under her watchful eye. She passed on to me her innate wisdom of gardening. I remember at a young age the emphasis she put on the importance of compost. She said, "If you spread compost in your garden you'll have healthy plants". In the last few decades scientists from all over the world are proving this point. I feel privileged that I learned in such a natural and loving way.

INDEX